NO OTHER WAY

Canada and International

Security Institutions

NO OTHER WAY

Canada and International Security Institutions

John W. Holmes

with contributions by
Ian Smart, Gabriel Warren, Leon Gordenker, W. H. Barton,
Michael Kergin, Robert Cameron, and Gerald Wright

Centre for International Studies

University of Toronto

ISBN 0-7727-0806-1

Canadian Cataloguing in Publication Data

Main entry under title:
No other way : Canada and international security institutions

Proceedings of a conference held in June 1984.
Includes bibliographical references and index.
ISBN 0-7727-0806-1

1. International agencies – Canada – Congresses. 2. Security, International – Congresses. 3. Canada – Foreign relations – 1945-   – Congresses. I. Holmes, John W., 1910-   . II. Smart, Ian. III. University of Toronto. Centre for International Studies.

JX1995.N6 1986   327.1'16   C86-094802-1

The Centre for International Studies
at the University of Toronto
was established in 1976 to promote
graduate studies and research in
international relations and
foreign area studies.

DIRECTOR: Professor Robert Spencer

Printed and bound in Canada by
T.H. Best Printing Co. Ltd., Don Mills, Ontario
Design: The Dragon's Eye Press, Toronto, Ontario
Typeset in Canada by Q Composition, Islington, Ontario

Contents

5 *NATO and Western Security* 99

6 *Conclusion: Security and Survival*
JOHN W. HOLMES 141

Foreword

Canada has long had the reputation internationally of being a 'good joiner.' A charter member of both the United Nations and the North Atlantic Treaty Organization (NATO) and also one of the two North American members of the Conference on Security and Co-operation in Europe (CSCE), Canada has played a major role in these and in a broader, complex web of international institutions. As Joe Clark, the Canadian secretary of state for external affairs, recently observed, Canada has learned that 'the real art in managing our current international relations resides in skilful deployment of our resources among all available channels – broad multilateral, plurilateral, bilateral.' 'We have,' he concluded, 'a tremendous stake in performing this balancing act well.'[1] In a problem-saturated world, Mr Clark's statement set Canada in line with what the United Nations secretary-general, Javier Pérez de Cuellar, has referred to as 'the essentiality of the multilateral approach to the solution of international problems.'[2] As Ian Smart puts it in the essay below, which contributed the title of this volume, there is 'no other way.'

In June 1984 the graduate Centre for International Studies at the University of Toronto organized a small expert conference to examine

Canada's perceptions of and role in international security institutions, as well as the nature, structure, and functions of these institutions themselves. The conference program featured a series of distinguished speakers from the ranks of both academe and officialdom, and the meeting attracted some seventy invited participants from universities across Canada and officials from Ottawa and elsewhere. In one respect at least the gathering was remarkable. For, as one non-Canadian speaker observed, to be able to bring together in one room specialists in both the United Nations and NATO was an achievement which it would be hard to duplicate elsewhere.

This volume is a product of that conference. It contains eight papers which were presented at it, together with an account of the discussions which followed and an analysis of the topics covered. While the papers have been revised, no attempt has been made to bring them up to date. They must be read essentially as statements delivered in mid-1984.

John Holmes, counsellor at the Canadian Institute of International Affairs, professor of political science in the University of Toronto, and a moving spirit behind the Centre's research program on international institutions, has made a twofold contribution to this volume. He is the sole author of the Introduction and of Chapter 3, which provided the background to the conference discussions; he is also responsible for the analysis of various aspects of the subject and for the Conclusion. Unlike the chapters of which he is sole author, these naturally reflect the discussion and incorporate the views of many speakers and participants.

Ian Smart, the author of Chapter 2, is currently an independent energy consultant in London, England; he is a former assistant director of the International Institute for Strategic Studies and a former director of studies of the Royal Institute of International Affairs. His chapter was delivered at the only public session of the conference and served as its keynote address. Gabriel Warren was, at the time of the conference, director-general of the Bureau of Multilateral Affairs at the Department of External Affairs, Ottawa. Leon Gordenker, the leading American scholar in the field, was professor at the Center for International Studies at Princeton University. William H. Barton, currently the chairman of the Board of Directors of the Canadian Institute for International Peace and Security, Ottawa, had a long career with the Department of External Affairs, during which he served as Canada's permanent representative to the United Nations, New York. Michael Kergin, recently appointed Canada's ambassador to Cuba, was at the time of the conference a senior member of the Canadian Permanent Mission to the United Nations, New York. Robert Cameron, formerly Canada's ambassador to Yugoslavia and to Poland and the German Democratic Republic, was assistant undersecretary of state for external affairs, in Ottawa, in charge of the Bureau of International Security and Arms Control. At the time of the conference he was foreign service visitor in the University of Toronto. Gerald Wright, vice-president of the Donner Canadian Foundation, was until 1985 president of the Atlantic Council of Canada. We were indebted to William Maynes, editor of *Foreign Policy*, who brought a perspective from Washington, and to the other participants and commentators: Margaret Doxey of Trent University, Rod Byers of York University, Harald von Riekhoff of Carleton University, Peter Dobell, director of the Parliamentary Centre for Foreign Policy and Foreign Trade, John Halstead, former Canadian ambassador to NATO, and Robert Reford, former director of the Canadian Institute of International Affairs and now president of the United Nations Association in Canada. The very able rapporteurs were Linda Goldthorp and Susan McDonald.

Many hands have gone into the making of *No Other Way*. In addition to the authors of papers presented at the conference and those who contributed in so significant a way to the discussions on which it was based, I should like to thank, above all, the Donner Canadian Foundation, which over a period of nearly eight years supported in a most generous fashion the Centre's study of Canada and international institutions and made possible both the conference on 14–15 June 1984 and the publication of this volume reporting on it. The Department of External Affairs co-operated with and supported the Centre, notably by providing a strong team of senior officials. Trinity College, University of Toronto, in whose quarters the Centre's offices are housed, made available once again its unrivalled facilities for the conference sessions. I should also like to express my thanks to Carlotta Lemieux for her expert editing, to Helen Mah for her attractive design, to Marion Magee, editor at the Canadian Institute of International Affairs, for her helpful advice, and especially to the former staff of the Centre for International Studies, Sandy Giles, Patti Johnstone, and Susan Grant, who helped in so many ways.

In preparing for the press a volume based on the proceedings of a conference held two years earlier, it is hard not to be struck by the continuities despite political change in Ottawa. In its first throne speech soon after taking office in September 1984, the government of Prime Minister Mulroney reiterated the familiar theme that 'Canada's opportunity to influence the course of world events lies primarily in sound multilateral institutions,' and a determination 'that Canada will again play its full part in the defence systems of NATO.'[3] More recently, the Report of the Special Joint Committee on Canada's International Relations dealt with many of the themes that were discussed in the Centre's conference held two years earlier. 'Almost all Canadians,' it reported, 'share a strong concern about international peace and security.... They supported continued participation in the North Atlantic Alliance and the assignment of Canadian forces to NATO commands.... Despite its deficiencies ... Canadians believe that the United Nations remains a necessary foundation for international order.'[4] It is hoped that this volume will contribute to an understanding of Canada's role in the two principal security organizations to which it belongs as well as in the newer and rather novel CSCE.

Robert Spencer
Trinity College
University of Toronto
September 1986

NOTES

1 Canada, Department of External Affairs, *Statement 86/30: Notes for a Speech by the Right Honourable Joe Clark, Secretary of State for External Affairs, at the Centre for International Studies, University of Toronto, 22 May 1986*, 2.
2 'Understanding the Requirements of Peace: The Intellectual's Responsibility,' *International Studies Newsletter* 13, no 5 (June/July 1986), 3.
3 Canada, House of Commons *Debates* (5 November 1984), 7.
4 *Interdependence and Internationalism: Report of a Special Joint Committee of the Senate and the House of Commons on Canada's International Relations* (June 1986), 9, 18.

Abbreviations

CCSBMDE	Conference on Confidence- and Security-Building Measures and Disarmament in Europe
CMEA	Council for Mutual Economic Assistance
CSCE	Conference on Security and Co-operation in Europe
EC	European Communities
ECOSOC	Economic and Social Council
GATT	General Agreement on Tariffs and Trade
IAEA	International Atomic Energy Agency
ICAO	International Civil Aviation Organization
IFAD	International Fund for Agricultural Development
IMF	International Monetary Fund
INF	Intermediate Nuclear Force
ITU	International Telecommunication Union
KAL	Korean Air Lines
MBFR	Mutual and Balanced Force Reductions
MNF	Multinational Force in Lebanon
NATO	North Atlantic Treaty Organization
NORAD	North American Aerospace Defence Command
NPG	Nuclear Planning Group

OAS	Organization of American States
OAU	Organization for African Unity
OECD	Organization for Economic Co-operation and Development
PJBD	Permanent Joint Board on Defence
PLO	Palestine Liberation Organization
SACEUR	Supreme Allied Commander Europe
SALT	Strategic Arms Limitation Talks
SDI	Strategic Defense Initiative
UNCTAD	United Nations Conference on Trade and Development
UNDOF	United Nations Disengagement Observer Force
UNDP	United Nations Development Programme
UNEF	United Nations Emergency Force
UNESCO	United Nations Educational, Scientific, and Cultural Organization
UNFICYP	United Nations Force in Cyprus
UNHCR	United Nations High Commissioner for Refugees
UNICEF	United Nations Children's Fund
UNIFIL	United Nations Interim Force in Lebanon
UNRWA	United Nations Relief and Works Agency for Palestine Refugees in the Near East
UNSSOD	United Nations Special Session on Disarmament
UNTSO	United Nations Truce Supervision Organization
WEO	Western European and Others group
WEU	Western European Union
WTO	Warsaw Treaty Organization (Warsaw Pact)

NO OTHER WAY

Canada and International

Security Institutions

JOHN W. HOLMES

1 Introduction

The peoples of the world, all of us in one way or another, feel insecure. Of course, people always have felt insecure and probably always will, but in the past their fears were less universal in scope. The causes of fear – economic, social, and military – are not hard to define, and it serves little purpose to scare ourselves to death, underlining our resolve with ever grimmer accounts of inevitable disaster. Prescriptions are elusive. It is customary to conclude dire analyses with the ringing statement that all that is lacking is the political will. This sounds appropriately sonorous, but it is a cop-out. First comes the hard question: 'The political will to do exactly what?' In an interdependent and intervulnerable world we have increasingly felt the need for some kind of structures which will recognize that conflicts of interest and conflicts of will are permanent parts of life itself. Are we losing faith in structures? Or are we just losing faith in the international institutions created since the last war?

In most criticisms there is an implied assumption that something else would work, that if our feckless United Nations, for example, does not work (whatever 'work' may mean), something structured in accordance with the critics' preferred view of global realities would.

Elimination of the veto in the Security Council would do the trick, or weighted voting; or more power to the General Assembly, or its abolition; or the privatization of the World Bank. The North Atlantic Treaty Organization would work if its members were forced to behave. However, the possibilities of altering the Charter of the United Nations or of amending the text of the North Atlantic Treaty by consent and in accordance with the rules of the game as toughly negotiated at birth are easily ignored by office-chair strategists. One does not pull plants up by the roots just because they are not as shapely as had been expected.

Is the loss of faith even deeper? As Ian Smart points out in the following chapter, we know of 'no other way' to seek an orderly world except through international institutions. Despondence is aggravated, however, by the knowledge that we have tried many ways with indifferent success so far. Never before, as Ian Smart points out, have there been so many institutions for peace and security. We have the mechanisms in place, but finding out how to make them work is extremely difficult. This basic fact is too often obscured by the search for villains, as if a few verdicts of guilty would show us the way. Simply determining who was responsible for the Cold War or the sad state of developing countries does not get us far, although it may cast some light on the problems. Conflicts are as often between right and right as between right and wrong. It is the perpetual predicament of an inevitably conflictual world and the intrinsic dilemmas of any and all institutions that must occupy our attention.

Do we lack the historical sense? Preoccupation with the notion of crisis diverts us from a proper awareness of evolving structures. Cynicism is dangerously fashionable, and the opinion makers too glibly ignore the enormous extent of what is in place and what has been accomplished over the past few centuries. Casting our minds back a century or two would make clear that the alternative to our hard-won internationalism is not realism, as claimed, but dog-eat-dogism, a swift slide into a new and much more densely populated Dark Age or into a still darker one that is not populated at all. It is not just the United Nations that is at stake; it is the habit of and instinct for international collaboration that we may be in danger of losing. It is not just the raucous General Assembly that is threatened but, along with it in all likelihood, those institutions that make possible international aviation, the checking of cholera or hijacking, the forestalling of a disastrous international financial collapse (as in 1982), or the simple passage of letters and telegrams beyond national frontiers. These are integral parts of the international system which has so laboriously been constructed.

It might be said that we are in danger of losing these things if we think we are. Leaders of many countries, including the most powerful, now pour scorn on what, through their tunnel vision, they call 'the UN'; but when the Reagan administration, contemptuous though it had been of the United Nations as an instrument through which peace could be established in the Middle East, found its extramural 'peacekeeping' in Lebanon a tragic miscalculation, voices were raised in Washington – and even in Paris, where the United Nations has rarely been favoured – asking why the United Nations should not assume this responsibility. It was salutary at least that the need for such a third force was recognized, even though the present disposition of majorities of the General Assembly and Security Council, aggravated by the failure of Western leadership, does raise legitimate doubts about how effectively such a force could serve the purpose at the moment.

Something like the United Nations remains essential even if it is not easily attainable. The aim, then, is not to renounce the United Nations system in all its breadth but to find ways of making it serve our purposes. Obviously, some elements work better than others and some are dispensable or ephemeral, but attention has to be paid to the health of the system. However dispensable UNESCO may seem to be, no one wants to pull out of the World Meteorological Organization or those other United Nations bodies which provide the essential infrastructure of an interdependent world so effectively that they are overlooked in the grand calculations about world order. Many international institutions serve useful purposes without direct attachment to the United Nations. Countries are going to pick and choose among institutions, but they also have to give and take.

It is not only the universal bodies that are viewed with cynicism. NATO is routinely deplored as being incapable of holding the Atlantic world together, but we have 'no other way' of co-ordinating the military activities and policies of large and small powers. The Conference on Security and Co-operation in Europe, established at Helsinki in 1973, has been regarded as a failure by both utopians and hard-liners because Europe is still divided, but none of the thirty-five participating states wants to abandon it. None of these structures is being employed to fulfil our best intentions, but we would have no place to go without them. The persistent question of whether the United Nations is doing a good job, which the simple-minded pollsters keep putting to their publics, puts the issue upside down. The United Nations cannot do anything; only its members can. International institutions are not ends in themselves; they are means to ends. They are not self-propelled; they have to be used with wisdom and foresight by member states.

The charter or rules of procedure of institutions that have any hope of success are not handed down on tablets from Mount Sinai or San Francisco. They have to be malleable, and most of them are. Growth is organic, and this involves, or should, not only new experiments but also the lopping off of limbs and even some replanting. Adaptability is all. Although international institutions have proliferated since 1945 (and proliferation is a sign of both health and excess), it is a mistake to assume that it all began with 1945. The chapters that follow are concerned not only with formal institutions but also with established ways and means, with habits and patterns of behaviour, with limitations on national actions, and with rules and regulations, norms, and international law. It is this 'webbed structure,' not all good or all bad and always in transition, that is undermined by the present disregard. In fear and panic, leaders and their publics are inclined to forget the awful importance of the precedents they set, even when they act in retaliation or are 'just doing what others are getting away with.' No country, of course, lives up to its commitments to the United Nations Charter, but persistently rejecting it as an accepted code speeds the unravelling of the order we seek to live by.

On the other hand, a preoccupation with theory can divert our attention from what might be done about specific issues. The practitioners, past and present, warn us against getting stalled on too high a level of generalities. Instead of being preoccupied with the 'roles' of the United Nations or of Canada, we should also ask, 'What do we do next?' or 'What precisely can we do in this situation?' There are things, they point out, that can actually be done about this issue or that, about this body or that, which would be missed if we adhered to all the generalizations about the art of the possible. Contemplating what is not generally feasible discourages efforts which might, in particular conflicts, deserve a good try. The argument is not just for short-range pragmatism but rather for the functional approach, with an eye to the consequences of action, wary about precedents set, but recognizing that international structures have developed more soundly by doing things than by the holding of constitutional conventions.

There exists now a galaxy of international institutions, governmental and non-governmental, regional and universal, or nearly so, that is nothing like the hierarchical system of 'world government' envisaged by the utopians in the first half of the century. There is no cabinet and no legislature. We have learned to take a functional approach to institutions, pragmatically developing ways and means of coping with perceived problems rather than seeking to impose a philosopher's dream. It is undoubtedly the only possible way to 'manage' a globe that is anything but uniform. So far, so good, but complacency is the risk in functionalism. The best we can manage may not be good enough. The paradox we have to live with is that although the mere survival of a populated globe, in face of the threat of pollution, depletion of resources, and changing climate, seems to require a global disciplinary authority, schemes for such a body have had to be dismissed as political-science fiction. As we still grope for ways of restraining war, the non-military threats to our security, to our very survival, become more urgent. One might hope that the urgency will in time expose the basic idiocy of the military confrontations from which we suffer. Meanwhile, for peace and security we have to look to the international institutions which exist, or which might conceivably be established by consensus.

IAN SMART

2 The International System: Will Chaos or Order Prevail?

Some years ago, one of the many distinguished economists 'south of the border' castigated his professional colleagues for using their talents, as he put it, to optimize the arrangement of deck chairs on the *Titanic*. By that token, if I write here of order within a singular international system as something imaginable, I may well be accused of addressing passengers in the saloon of that same lamented steamer on the proposition that icebergs are made of marshmallow. To lecture while the ship sinks may be thought no worse than to chatter while the world plunges towards apparent anarchy.

Treating international security in the simplest and most conventional manner, as equated with peace and military safety, the prospect is clearly a dismal one. To quote a recent edition of the *Strategic Survey* from the International Institute for Strategic Studies:

There were more problems and crises during 1983 than any progress towards solutions.... Wars continued to rage in Lebanon, the Persian Gulf, Afghanistan, Southern Africa, Central America, Kampuchea and other areas of the developing world. In few, if any, of these conflicts ... could it be claimed that a settlement was significantly nearer than it had been at the end of 1982, despite the loss of many thousands of lives and the expenditure of billions of dollars.[1]

Still more worryingly, as many of us would see it *Strategic Survey* noted the continuing and apparently wilful lowering of the temperature between the United States and the Soviet Union: an ulcerous depression, threatening 'to become a deep, enduring, systemic trough.'[2] The probability of general nuclear war between the two superpowers and their alliances, which would mark the end of our modern world, is still, I believe, extremely small. But I also fear that the behaviour of their governments has recently conspired to make such a war more nearly conceivable than at any time in more than twenty years.

A broader, less conventional but, arguably, more useful view of human security would look beyond the military relationships between sovereign nations to embrace physical welfare at every level. Sadly, taking such a view may lead to an equally depressing conclusion. To war and the threat of war among states we must then add the blight of serious intercommunal violence, from India and Ireland to central Africa and the Philippines. We must next recount the sordid catalogue of terrorism (which I take to involve a gratuitous preference for using force in pursuit of a political end). We must then raise our eyes from physical violence alone to see also those non-violent symptoms of economic or societal malaise, marking the divisions that give the lie to any idea of a homogeneous international system: symptoms of poverty, disease, hunger, unemployment, and indebtedness, with their counterparts of international competition and conflict over resources, trade, and the management of financial assets. For the larger part of humanity, the only alternative to a violent death may seem to be a life dominated, irreparably marred, and probably shortened by the ignorance, avarice, or self-protective exigence of their more fortunate fellows.

It may be argued that my portrait of the world is a travesty, that it distorts by ignoring everything except violence, suffering, and the accompanying sense of danger. So it may. But we shall do well to begin by facing the truth that within our own generation, our species has made little or no progress towards eliminating these phenomena. Looking around us, we must recognize that there is a rising tide of genuine fear and incipient despair in most of our societies: real fear of economic deprivation, social disruption, or nuclear disaster, a fear that is vastly exacerbated by a sense of powerlessness to avoid such outcomes.

Of course, there are other features of the world to see – brighter features of notable achievement and hopeful expectation. But the shadows have grown long enough and deep enough in the last decade to persuade many that talking about a prospect of order in the international system is either impossible or, if possible, irrelevant. Nor is hope likely to be rekindled merely by observing that international organizations dedicated to security, order, harmony and progress have proliferated even as the gloom has gathered.

Never in recorded history have the world's inhabitants and governments been equipped with anything like so broad an array of global and regional institutions for protecting human security, for solving human problems, and for resolving human conflicts. Yet international relations have rarely seemed more darkly shaded by uncertainty, intractability, and intransigence. We have provided ourselves richly with the institutional apparatus of an ordered world, but this seems to have brought us no closer to the reality. Evidently, we know no other way of trying to achieve order at the international level than by labouring to build, sustain, and work collectively through institutions, whether they be quasi-permanent intergovernmental organizations or more ephemeral conferences. On the face of it, therefore, since our failures are in despite of our best endeavours, our despondency is doubly justified.

Because I believe all this, I may seem to be merely perverse if I go on to display any remnant of optimism. Nevertheless, this is what I intend to do, for I have not convinced myself of doom. To be sure, the picture I have sketched is accurate; our prevalent image of an increasingly disorderly and dangerous world is well founded in observation. But the picture is unfinished, the observation sometimes too superficial and often too narrowly focused. To be more specific, I submit that what has so far been painted suffers from at least four deficiencies. In the first place, it is a caricature, achieving part of its effect by leaving out significant features of even the superficially apparent reality. In the second place, the perspective is distorted. The artist has not fully understood the interplay of forces bearing on what we are pleased to call the system of international politics. Thirdly, it lacks a clear and dominant focus. Whoever painted it was confused about the goals of international policy, and particularly the goal of order itself. Fourthly, as a direct result, the picture is defective in composition. It fails to place the figure of international organization in a position appropriate to the role that it should in fact play. It is these deficiencies, therefore, that I seek to repair in the following pages.

The problem of caricature is probably the easiest to resolve. Our world is punctuated by conflict, violence, and suffering, and their occurrence inevitably captures immediate attention. Yet, as Sherlock Holmes knew, the more important fragment of evidence may be the dog that does not bark. Some 'dogs' that used to be noisy have fallen silent during our lifetime. Without trying to tell them over, let me offer two very different examples to illustrate their number.

In many parts of the market economies in the Organization for Economic Co-operation and Development (OECD), and especially in manufacturing industry, we are facing a crisis of employment – or, rather, of unemployment. I say crisis, a word I do not use lightly, because the reversible effects of a cyclical recession, analogous to that of the 1930s, seem partly to be concealing a more fundamental erosion of employment, caused by the warping of aged industrial and social structures under the stress of rapid technological change: a theme to which I shall return. Economic recovery may in fact accelerate this erosion, rather than halt it. It was the human cost of prolonged unemployment that contributed in the 1930s to the rise of National Socialism in Germany, as it had contributed in the 1840s to an internationalization of social and political ferment throughout Europe. Since World War II, however, the individual cost of unemployment has been enormously reduced, in most Western countries, by national social welfare provisions which would not all have been possible without the mechanisms of international monetary adjustment. The result is an extraordinary, if far from perfect, silence. By the standards of earlier generations, it is inconceivable that recent and current levels of unemployment would not again have generated domestic disorder and political upheaval on a scale whose effects, especially in Europe, would have reached across national frontiers. Yet in the 1980s, despite the deeply critical nature of the situation, this dog has yet to bark.

At a totally different point on the political spectrum, a similar effect seems to have flowed from very different causes in the case of war between states. We see, all too vividly, the persistence of war as an instrument of national policy in Asia, Africa, Latin America, and the Middle East. What we do not see is war between industrial nations: between the superpowers or, most notably, between the states of Europe. During all the centuries from the Middle Ages to 1945, Europe was notoriously the region that was most prolific in organized international violence. Forty years without some deliberate, large-scale use of military force between European nations is a circumstance almost without precedent since those nations first existed. True, we have had some narrow escapes in the last four decades. But the fact remains that war, as such, has become a stranger to the European environment in which it flourished for so long, even though the policies and purposes of the European nations are still as far from coinciding as they were in the nineteenth century. Trieste, Berlin, the Sud Tirol, the Atlantic fisheries – any of these and other recent disputes among Europeans might then have been a sufficient *casus belli*. None has had that outcome since 1945. Nor has war entered as a newcomer during these years into the Soviet-American relationship, despite the enormous strains imposed by irreconcilable ideologies, incompatible state interests, and specific conflicts in places as far apart as the Caribbean, the Middle East, and Indochina. These are not benefits to be ignored or taken for granted. Again, earlier generations would have expected military force to be used in an effort to resolve a number of the crises and conflicts of interest that have arisen between the superpowers or in Europe since World War II. As with the rough hounds of revolution, however, this dog has so far only growled.

What does this necessarily negative evidence suggest? The popular perception is that direct use of military force has been avoided between the superpowers largely, if not wholly, because they possess nuclear weapons. Equally, it is believed that Europe's unprecedented experience of regional peace owes much to the corollaries of that inhibited relationship between the superpowers: to the Soviet subjugation of Eastern Europe, to the United States' guarantee of Western Europe's security, and to the different but complementary disciplines thus imposed on any impulse to national belligerence in the European continent. Reassured as well as shackled by this discipline, the Europeans have themselves made real progress towards harmonizing conflicting interests and codifying their avoidance of warfare, most notably in the European Communities (EC) but also by such means as the Helsinki Final Act of 1975. In the first instance, however, relative peace among the industrial nations of East and West has been the Faustian reward of a nuclear age; or so received wisdom would have it.

The truth may be more complicated. But initially I am less concerned to scrutinize a conventional explanation than to note the phenomenon of peace among the traditionally strong and to explore its implications for the balance between order and chaos. For example, it is important to recognize that the negative evidence I have adduced in and among industrial countries – the muted dogs – offsets the earlier catalogue of violent conflict in what we now call the Third World. The net effect is that, setting aside short-term fluctuations, there is surprisingly little sign that the world of nation states, viewed as a whole, has become more prone to violence. The focus of military conflict has shifted towards less industrialized regions, but its global frequency has hardly altered. There have been important increases in the costs of warfare, as a result of technical change, but technology has not yet caused recourse to war to become more commonplace. All in all, the idea that our world or that of our children must be seen as more chaotically violent than the world of fifty – or two hundred – years ago will not stand up to scrutiny.

We are only one of many generations that have believed themselves beset by unprecedented violence. But we should not exaggerate our predicament. The traditional and convenient idea of an international system continues to refer, as it always has done, to an intricate web of conflicting and converging national interests and aspirations. The tension in different parts of this uneven fabric continues to vary over time, and the apparent cost effectiveness of alternative instruments of national policy (including moral guilt among the costs) continues to dominate decisions about their use. Consequently, war is still used between states whenever some government sees reason to expect a net benefit from using it, but not otherwise. If the frequency of highly organized violence is to be our criterion of chaos in the international system, as it often has been, then a view across the present and prospective world as a whole reveals little real change. The pattern of chaos and order is still a shifting global kaleidoscope in which neither element decisively predominates. As a historian, I would have to conclude that the answer to the question in my title – 'Will chaos or order prevail?' – is 'No.' To this extent, I must be regarded as a qualified optimist.

For good or ill, this is only the beginning of the story, not the end. Internationally, the ratio of order to chaos, peace to war, may not obviously be changing by conventional standards, but the distribution and style of international violence are certainly changing. Most clearly, as we have seen, the principal arena of violent interstate conflict has been shifting from the highly developed regions of the northern temperate zone to less developed tropical and subtropical battlegrounds. This shift needs an explanation.

One reason commonly given for the change of geographical focus is that new nations created by decolonization are naturally under special pressure to assert their newfound sovereignty – to define its reach, demonstrate its legitimacy, defend its existence – and that such pressure militates in favour of more abrasive and violent conflict, internationally and internally, whenever sovereignty seems to be challenged. Another and more sinister allegation is that the Third World has, in some measure, become the field for violent conflict by proxy on the part of older and more developed nations, especially the superpowers. Evidence supporting each of these explanations can be drawn from appropriate cases. Even in combination, the implication that Third World states include a preponderance of aggressive adolescents who are nevertheless readily available as compliant puppets does not entirely satisfy me. In any case, the reasons offered have more to do with the contamination by violent conflict of the Third World than with progressively less violent relations among industrialized states.

I have already expressed some scepticism about the most popular explanation of the latter phenomenon. As everyone recognizes, among the most highly developed countries, the expected cost of engaging in war has risen since 1945, especially because of the nuclear options now available. Yet I believe that it is misleading to look only at costs. No less important is the fact that the benefits those countries can reasonably expect to obtain from avoiding war have also increased. In the first place, the material rewards of international technical and industrial collaboration by advanced countries have arguably risen.

In the second place, the governments of those states have been able to choose from a growing range of non-military means to pursue and to reconcile their national interests. Access to those rewards and opportunities naturally entails avoiding violent conflict. Thus, the actual benefits of remaining at peace have added a growing weight, in the policy balance, to the probable costs of engaging in war.

It is hardly necessary to emphasize the role of international organizations in this process. Such selectively focused institutions as the OECD and the EC, the economic summits and the Bank for International Settlements, have come to play a vital part as mechanisms for pursuing national goals or resolving disputes without resort to war, just as other international bodies such as NATO have played a part in sustaining the expected cost of war itself. One of the features of the international scene since World War II has been the multiplication of organizations dedicated to joint action by similarly circumstanced governments in order to maximize the rewards of peace or the penalties of war. What needs to be emphasized, however, is that the scope of such organizations has hitherto been strongly biased towards the industrial world.

I do not scorn the work done in or on behalf of the Third World by United Nations agencies or national aid administrations. Nor do I mean to diminish the importance of Third World contributions to global bodies that are concerned with finance, trade, or social development. But I note that within the Third World, there are only a few true analogues of indigenous groupings such as the OECD, or the Council for Mutual Economic Assistance (CMEA), and that the absence of Third World analogues is especially obvious in regions where violent international conflict remains endemic, such as in the Middle East. Those organizations that do exist stand out: the Association of South East Asian Nations (ASEAN), for example, and the Andean Pact. Neither separately nor in the aggregate, however, are these fragments of multilateral machinery for peaceful collaboration yet remotely comparable to the older, stronger, and more numerous organizations at the disposal of the industrialized economies. Nor, it must be added, is the Third World yet endowed with institutions for crisis management or conflict resolution that can be compared even with these flimsy bridges across the gulf between East and West.

The existence of appropriate multilateral institutions is not, of course, the only reason why war has gone out of fashion among developed countries. However, the very different situation in the Third World adds some colour to a related proposition: that interstate violence in the South is unlikely to diminish to the level now familiar in the industrial North until the material benefits of peace have been substantially increased there as well. The recent preference in the industrial world for avoiding war can be attributed not only to the stick of military deterrence in a nuclear age but also to the carrot of profitable international co-operation, especially in economics and technology. We would all wish that other areas of the world, where violent conflict remains familiar, would develop a similar preference for peace without having to rely solely on the deterrent influence of expensive military sticks – still less on a nuclear bludgeon. In this case, more must surely be done towards a collaborative cultivation of the carrots. In the South, as in the North, war will not finally be rejected until peace has made an offer that cannot be refused.

Into these last remarks there slipped an oblique reference to technology as a field for international collaboration. But technology has a larger and very different relevance to our subject. I suggested earlier that the conventional picture of the present international system suffered not only from caricature but also from a failure to understand the contemporary pressures on international order: a deficiency of perspective. This is where technology re-enters the scene.

Quite deliberately, I have so far adopted the practice of equating international order with peace and of equating international chaos with violence and war. Although this practice is hallowed by age, I believe it to be dangerous. In the final analysis, war has never in fact been the autogenous enemy of world order. What it has always been is an effect, an expression, and thus an indicator, of order's subversion by its true enemies; that is, by the conflicts among nations from which war has arisen and to resolve which war has been chosen. This distinction between cause and effect is not mere pedantry. Keeping hold of the difference between conflict itself and the violence that conflict sometimes – but only sometimes – provokes is central to understanding order in human affairs, and especially to understanding how, when, and why order gives way to chaos.

Territorial, ideological, and economic conflicts have always lain at the root of wars. Violence has sometimes resolved these conflicts.

Just as often it has exacerbated them. Most frequently, it has done no more than alter their form or else force them into different channels. In all cases, the conflict has existed independently of the war. Historically, of course, wars have conveniently indicated the seriousness of conflicts between states; but as I noted earlier, among the industrial states of the northern hemisphere their usefulness as an indicator has greatly diminished during the last half century. Herein lies the danger, for the incidence of organized violence between nations no longer even approximately measures the severity of their conflicts, still less the ratio of social and political chaos to international order. Consequently, to persist in the habit of basing such measurements only on the observation of international violence carries with it a considerable risk of self-delusion.

The error would be to suppose that, just because the costs of war and the benefits of peace have both increased, the underlying conflicts of interest or policy between developed countries have become fewer or less serious. In reality, despite some moderation of historical rivalries in Western Europe, our so-called international system continues to be defaced by an abundance of conflicts, offering a largely undiminished resistance to the forces of order. Within the industrial world, the relative importance of strictly territorial disputes may have declined since 1945, but the number and severity of ideological conflicts have not decreased. Meanwhile, economic divergences and fears have steadily multiplied.

There is nothing new in a multiplicity of international economic conflicts. Many of those we have recently encountered (over the terms for access to natural resources such as oil, or over the restriction of trade and the protection of national markets) are only the latest representatives of a rich tradition. What has increased is the variety of international economic conflict. Since the 1940s, for example, we have had to become more inured to open conflict over monetary policy and exchange rates. More recently, and more worryingly, we have had to face a rising tide of conflict over the international repercussions of national economic strategies – as, for instance, with the use of high interest rates by one country to suck in the funds with which to support a chronic budgetary deficit. We are now, I believe, moving on another front into a period when conflicts of the traditional kind over international trade will progressively be augmented and even overshadowed by conflicts about industrial policy and the international location of manufacturing capacity. All in all, therefore, the agenda of economic conflict between industrial countries, or even among OECD members alone, has become steadily longer during a period of peace, and the effects of these conflicts have become more pervasive.

This is a part of the background to the emerging role of technology in shaping the balance between international order and chaos; for technical progress and change are obviously and closely associated with many of the economic conflicts just mentioned, sometimes to the extent of aggravating an international divergence and occasionally even to the point of causing one. During the last few years, we have come to know one example in the West, in the shape of conflict over transmitting high technology to the Soviet Union. In particular fields – computer design, for instance, or the technology of nuclear energy – dissent over trade in technical knowledge or equipment has long been familiar.

All these cases, in which technology overtly provides subject matter for international conflict, are only the most superficial evidence of a much larger problem. One level below the surface, we find changing technology serving not as a subject for international conflict but as a source of the mechanisms by which conflicts are stimulated, prosecuted, or constrained. Patently, the technology of violence itself, from handguns to hydrogen bombs, has played all of these roles. Because the relationship is less brutally obtrusive, we may sometimes forget the parallel part played by the evolving technologies of communication and information handling. It is not only that mass communication through the public media broadcasts the sights and sounds of violence to a global audience. It is also that the ostensibly closed circuits of modern communication, together with the surveillance which opens them, offer both the enemies and defenders of order unprecedentedly efficient means of promoting, exploiting, or trying to contain social and political friction. Furthermore, the same methods of high-speed global communication, backed up by an even wider spectrum of information technologies, serve to transmit and amplify economic stress, as when co-ordinated speculation or alarm covering a global network of markets reinforces the volatility of exchange rates or commodity prices.

Two aspects of this deeper connection between technology and conflict seem to deserve an added emphasis. First, it is worth remarking that at this level there is little sign of technical change or progress affecting the human propensity for engaging in conflict. What is apparent instead is that technology has progressively magnified the direct effects and indirect repercussions of conflict. In other words, technical development, whether relating to force or information, has tended to increase the casualty occasioned internationally by conflict and thus to increase the cost. Second, it is important to notice that technical progress across the whole of the field discussed has had the effect of reducing characteristic differences between the capacities of different actors to initiate conflict, to control or influence its evolution, or to resolve it. As military technology advances, endowing progressively smaller weapons with progressively larger range and destructive power, so lesser nations or even guerrilla groups can offer a growing local threat to far greater states. As communications and information technology advances in its persistent search for more compact and cheaper systems, so the traditionally weaker antagonist – the small country, the guerrilla, the criminal, the individual speculator – can match or overmatch an ostensibly stronger adversary by competing on technically equal terms in intelligence, planning, and co-ordination. On the one hand, therefore, technology has exerted a profoundly egalitarian influence on the proportionality of conflicting strengths, just as it has considerably enhanced, on the other hand, the potential cost of engaging in conflict.

Neither of these links between technology and conflict is simple in pattern or unambiguous in its effects. Neither has yet received due attention from politicians or political scientists. For our present purpose, I am inclined to believe that there is a yet deeper level on which the most considerable interaction of technology and conflict is to be sought. If we want to judge the longer-term influence of technical change on the balance between chaos and order, we should certainly look to how technology magnifies casualty and equalizes local strength, rather than looking only to its role as a subject of international dispute. But we should then look further, to the phenomena of change itself and to how the accelerating rate of technical change in the modern world, almost independently of the technologies involved, has imposed a growing strain on our societies and their institutions of order.

Although it must often be a matter of impression rather than measurement, we can easily visualize a set of curves that make up a graph of historical change in a variety of dimensions. Some are familiar: curves of population change, for example, or of material output, or of the extraction and conversion of natural resources. Let us visualize three particular curves sweeping across the human past. One plots the progress of science and technology. Another plots the evolution of organized societies – of social attitudes and relationships. The third depicts the way in which institutions for making and implementing essentially political decisions have adapted themselves to changing human needs.

If we harmonize the scales to which these curves are drawn, we shall notice that one or another of them sometimes rises or falls more sharply than the rest, as when the technological curve surged temporarily ahead of the others during the early stages of the Industrial Revolution in Europe. Such divergences, however, have proved ephemeral, so that the three curves, viewed in a longer historical perspective, have followed a broadly similar path; or, rather, they did so throughout almost the whole of recorded history until the last years of the nineteenth century. Since about 1900, the graph of scientific progress and technological change records an astounding acceleration. Social attitudes and relationships have also been reformed in this period at an unprecedented rate, but at a rate far slower than that of technical change – as witness the traumas caused by our present crisis of structural unemployment in the West. Meanwhile, the rate of institutional adaptation in allegedly advanced societies seems, by comparison, to have increased hardly at all. As a result, we are moving towards the end of a century in which these three impressionistically plotted curves appear to have diverged, for the first time, in much more than an ephemeral way; and their divergence both records and signals the fact that technology has progressively been bursting the bounds of societal consensus and, above all, that technical change and social adaptation have alike been escaping from the grasp of political institutions.

This, I submit, is how technology now presents an issue that is not merely important to the future balance of order and chaos in human affairs, between nations and within them, but is actually crucial to it. We can readily identify specific cases where scientific or technical developments have become the focuses for social disquiet or political disagreement. Nuclear power might be one example, genetic engineering or the generation of acid rain another. I have argued in passing that such particular bones of contention are less germane to international order in the longer term than technology's contributions to increasing the damage that conflict can cause or technology's role in closing gaps of local strength between adversaries. My major contention, however, is that none of these considerations comes close to matching the foreseeable significance for social and political order of the sheer pace at which science and technology have been changing throughout this century, especially in relation to contemporaneous rates of social adjustment and institutional adaptation.

Perhaps more than any other process at a similar level of generality, the widening gaps between these historically concurrent processes of change threaten to destroy any remnant or prospect of order in human affairs. Certainly, in terms of psychological and political stress, I would now expect the divergence to endanger both international and internal security at least as much as any prospect or fear of military aggression.

In the cases where some sense of this danger has recently bubbled to the surface of politics – cases such as those just mentioned of nuclear power or genetic engineering – the most frequent reaction in the industrial West has been to call for additional political restrictions on the pace or direction of the offending technology's development. At the extreme, passionate arguments are advanced for halting, or even reversing, technical change. Because the underlying problem is the systematic divergence just described, this reaction is readily understandable. For the same reason, as we know well, it is also a reaction that is calculated to generate the maximum contention and confusion while achieving only very small fragments of the desired effect. In any case, and above all, it is ill-conceived.

The real problem, it might be argued, is not so much the extraordinary acceleration of technical change over almost a century; it is the failure of societal adaptation, and still more of institutional evolution, to keep pace. Our great-grandparents could afford to base their timetable for institutional development on inherited social wisdom and to assume that the rhythm of social adjustment moved to a generational metronome. In spite of – or perhaps because of – a rising concern about social revolution, their successors throughout the developed world, West and East, have clung to this faith in the durability of legislative, executive, and judicial structures. Meanwhile, the societal pressures generated by changing technology have rarely been considered at all. The result is that we are forced today to contemplate the imminent prospect of coping with the monstrous strain imposed by twenty-first-century technology on, at best, a mid-twentieth-century social consensus, with little but institutions handed down from the eighteenth and nineteenth centuries to preserve us from social or political collapse.

No one can reasonably argue that every use of the new opportunities offered by advancing science and technology is axiomatically and universally beneficial. Thus, no one can argue against all politically determined restrictions on how technology is applied. However, in sum, scientific and technical change has made a strongly positive contribution to human welfare. It is therefore self-destructive as well as futile to call only for policies which might drag the pace of that constantly accelerating process down to the far slower rate at which we have found it comfortable to modify our social attitudes; or even worse, to try to reduce it to match the almost imperceptible mutation of our state institutions. The challenge is not to halt technical change but to adapt to it, politically and socially. This requires that we regulate technical change, as we have always done; but it also requires that we stimulate societal and, above all, institutional change, as we have never done.

It is particularly because it reflected a superficial and trivialized view of the relation between technical change and political order that I have criticized my own original portrait of the world on the grounds of its faulty perspective. Moreover, an exploration of the issues that are presented by evolving technology has the added merit of carrying the discussion forward into the area covered by my third criticism of the painting, namely that it lacks a clear focus; that is, it lacks a clear view of the goals at which international policy should aim. The main problem here is that the concept of order is notably imprecise, or at least that it has been used all too carelessly. Often, for example, the goal of guarding order against the threat of chaos – or, as it is then labelled, of preserving stability – has been proclaimed as though it were tantamount to holding unaltered the prevailing international *status quo.* One lesson to be learned from thinking about the advance of technology is that obstinate efforts merely to stem the tide of change are doomed to fail eventually and that they are likely in the interim to provoke dissent, rather than to procure anything identifiable as order. The only useful interpretation of this last concept turns out to be in terms of successful adaptation. In other words, order is only to be secured or sustained by fitting political and other institutions for the task of guiding technical and social change along convergent paths.

Thus it is with technology. So it is also with political and strategic change in international affairs. If only to avoid yet another long excursion into the latter dimensions, I would refer diffidently at this point to a thesis propounded in a retrospective article for the *International Journal* on changing assumptions about international relations over twenty-five years. I wrote there of a sea-change in East-West relations, from entrenchment to manoeuvre, of related change in the bonds and patterns of alignment in the West, involving the relegation of military security as an organizing principle, of a more widespread reaffirmation of nationalism and the primacy of the nation state, of a deeply reaching erosion of international hierarchies, and, finally, of an apparent shift in the meaning of power itself. I concluded with the following words: 'Without the traditional organizing focus of ... a visible and unambiguous hierarchy, the assumptions of structural simplicity which still prevailed in the 1950s have given way to the image of a more mobile and untidy world, populated by more assertive but less confident states whose larger opportunities for manoeuvre do not always console them for the international system's loss of clarity.'[3] This is not the description of a politically or strategically changeless world. It is not even the description of a stable world, as commonly conceived. It is, in fact, the picture of a world – or an international system – where widespread and, arguably, intensifying political and strategic changes over twenty-five years have put cumulative pressure on international security, peace, and order, not least among industrial countries. It is a world in which, during that period, the number and gravity of the conflicts of interest and policy among those nations have not obviously altered, while their variety has increased. Yet it is still the world in which, as we saw earlier, the overall balance between order and chaos, measured by conventional standards, has not much changed and in which the use of organized violence among developed countries has actually become a vanishing rarity.

This earlier discussion did something to resolve what might otherwise have seemed a paradox. The persistence and diversification of conflict between industrial states, coupled with the rash of wars in the Third World, made up a less than orderly international system, within which the divergence of technical, social, and institutional change posed an increasingly serious long-term threat. But among developed countries the probable costs of war and the possible benefits of peace had simultaneously increased. Although this can only be the sketch of an explanation, we should not be astonished, therefore, to find that the world has become 'more mobile and untidy' without also becoming more violent overall. What has yet to be explained is why international relations in a world of such various and abrasive conflicts have not more obviously degenerated, even without greater violence. How is it that a more general breakdown of political order has been avoided in an international system that has been plagued for so long by strategic, economic, and ideological turmoil?

Our look at technology suggests that preserving even the semblance of order in international politics demands some collective success in adapting to changes of international adversity and alignment. In a world riven by such ideological, military, and economic differences, how has this kind of adaptation been possible? The answer, I believe, is that the considerable diversification of international conflict and, in many cases, its no less considerable aggravation, have been offset by a rarely acknowledged but equally significant modification in the norms of international behaviour. Taking the world as a whole, unresolved conflicts at the international level now set at odds a greatly increased number of sovereign states and non-national groups, confronting each other in a world where traditional alignments have been attenuated and traditional bases and patterns of power fragmented. Nevertheless, for reasons as numerous as they are ill-understood (reasons ranging from the costs of war and benefits of war-avoidance to an elusive but pervasive reinforcement of the cultural inhibitions on an overt external use of violence by the state), these more numerous conflicts and confrontations have more often been pursued without war. Still more important is the fact that despite all that has been done by technology and human ingenuity to enrich the available armoury of civil as well as military coercion, the non-violent tactics used to pursue conflict internationally, even between avowed adversaries, have been increasingly constrained by a network of tacit, even more than explicit, rules.

To argue this thesis in detail would obviously take too long. Suffice it to say that it can, I believe, be supported by persuasive evidence from recent years. The indication is that a large part of the responsibility for maintaining, since World War II, a relatively even global balance between what we have labelled 'order' and 'chaos' must be ascribed to the fact that the expanding membership of an increasingly incoherent system has nevertheless connived at an erratic, partly unconscious, but remarkable reinforcement of the effective limits on international behaviour. But what is immediately just as important, recalling the need for a clearly defined policy goal, is the further implication that the concept of order in an international system must itself be defined and differentiated with unusual care. We found earlier that creating or sustaining order presupposes a capacity not to resist changes but to harmonize change in different contexts. We now find that the order to which those who make international policy apparently aspire has at least three very different implicit connotations.

In the first place, there is the idea of a system that is orderly in its composition: one that is populated by a clearly delimited and reasonably homogeneous group of members, interconnected by a reasonably stable and well-understood network of relationships. The larger part of the international system had something of this character before 1914 but now retains nothing more than its remnants. In the second place, there is order as a relative measure of the frequency, strength, and predictability with which the interests of the system's members, as they understand them, converge, diverge, conflict, or run in parallel. As we have seen, there is little sign of a recent tendency towards greater global order by this criterion. In the third place, however, there is the sense of order as an index of generally accepted normative limits on how those in the system behave towards each other in pursuing their various interests: a measure possibly influenced by trends in the system's membership or by the dynamic interplay of interests, but eventually distinguishable from both. It is only by this third standard of international behaviour that there is much recent evidence to offset the gloom-ridden prognoses of chaos with which we began.

It would, of course, be foolish to suppose that the different versions of order are never connected. Even when given an ethical gloss, norms of behaviour, for instance, may owe a good deal to how a convergence or divergence of interests has affected the expected costs of alternative tactics. It should nevertheless be obvious that ignoring the distinctions between ordered membership of the international system, ordered interests, and ordered behaviour can easily lead to error, and the error can afflict policy as easily as it can afflict analysis. Unless those who make and execute international policy are meticulously clear about the particular version of order at which they aim – assuming that order in any form is among their goals – their policies, even if successful in one context, may unwittingly generate disorder in another.

The danger can be illustrated by observing one of the ways in which international politics have moved in recent years. The essay quoted earlier, on assumptions in international relations, made the point that there had been a noticeable tendency, especially in the West, to reassert the exclusive right of nation states and their governments to occupy the pinnacles of the international system, in defiance of supranationalist claims from above and transnationalist challenges from below. This reassertion of traditional status is readily represented as a contribution to regenerating order in the international system, by clarifying rights and by simplifying the distribution of political authority.[4] In reality, however, the sense of order that it addresses relates only to membership in the system, to the exclusion of promoting ordered patterns of interest or norms of behaviour. There is good reason for thinking that one effect is actually to provoke less 'orderly' behaviour on the part of some non-state entities – political and economic interest groups, or even international agencies – which are driven to resist an apparent attempt to diminish their own international status.

There are still stronger and more worrying reasons for believing that current reassertions of state nationalism may be taken to require or license increasingly abrasive or demonstratively exigent international behaviour by the national governments concerned. At the least, efforts to recapture acknowledged international primacy for the state have coincided with harsher restrictions on exports (as of high technology), tighter protection of national markets, and more selfish national attitudes to macroeconomic management and monetary policy. Although the inhibitions on violence between advanced countries have survived, some of their governments, arguably intent on demonstrating the unique virility of the state in strategic affairs as well, have given way to international outbursts of political or military adventurism, directed against supposed challenges by non-state groups in such peripheral areas as Afghanistan or El Salvador. All too clearly, therefore, actions taken in the name of that international order which measures systemic membership can cut across any tendency towards more ordered international behaviour and can easily jeopardize efforts to reconcile interests.

It is significant that this example has again pointed towards a conclusion similar to that reached earlier when considering the long-term political impact of scientific and technical change. The message is that policies which are consciously or unconsciously directed at halting change, as an end in itself, are not likely in the long run to serve the cause of international order. There is often an inclination to equate order with the preservation of the *status quo*, or with such impalpable idols as 'stability' – an inclination to which those who feel threatened by the forces of change are understandably prone. The tendency is encouraged by the brazen advertisement in some quarters of a conviction that all social, political, or ethical change is necessarily good – a view even more ludicrous than its antithesis. Neither of these extreme attitudes to change is tolerable.

In itself, change is neither good nor evil; but at every level of politics we must cope with the constant and characteristic, if occasionally naive, hunger of our species for material and spiritual improvement. There is no way to satisfy or even slightly assuage this hunger except through political, social, economic, and technical change. A steady flow of evidence that prudent change is in train, or at least that it is imminent, is necessary to any sense of human satisfaction; and some measure of human satisfaction, moderating both perceptions of interest and choices of behaviour, is as necessary to order at the international level as it is in our personal or domestic affairs. It is not, then, that all change is conducive to international order. Far from it. Change must still be wisely conceived and conducted. But it is certainly true that obstinate resistance to all change, albeit in the name of order, is a sure guarantee of eventual chaos.

Building on this reflection, we can at last set about repairing the deficiency of focus in our original portrait of the world, by defining more sharply the goal of international order. We may not be able to distil its ultimate essence; but having remarked on diverse and even incompatible versions of the concept, we can accept that any purely static image of international order is unlikely to yield good policy. Given human nature and the persistent expansion of human knowledge, order must usefully be regarded as a dynamic process of adaptation. It is in fact analogous to, as well as linked to, the concept of security in human affairs, which is too often assumed to be static but is really and essentially dynamic, just because security can only be measured by reference to a constantly evolving societal consensus about values. In much the same way, order as a goal of international politics must both reflect dynamic social views on technical and institutional change and be reflected in the dynamics of international behaviour.

A much looser but more provocative analogy might be taken from the natural sciences, and specifically from thermodynamics. Within our universe, the aggregate of energy is classically constant. Human beings have always had to exploit this finite stock in order to meet their individual needs and to satisfy their hunger for communal improvement. They can only extract utility from energy, however, by converting it from one form to another. Because each conversion involves some increase in entropy (that is, in disorder or chaos), the net effect is to feed rising entropy in the universe as a whole: an inexorable tendency of the system to which human choices admittedly make only an insignificant contribution, but from which they cannot escape. All that human beings can do is to ensure that their energy-converting activity is itself, in some sense, well ordered and that it serves orderly social and economic purposes, with political order as an ulterior goal. While such an impressionistic parallel should not be pressed too far, it does help to underline our sobering conclusions: that disorder is a natural condition, that change is essential to human purposes, that political and social order can only be secured by constant and intelligent management of change, and that order's most destructive enemies include, as a result, not only chaos but also, at the opposite pole, policies of immobilism. The primary task of politics, therefore, is to build and maintain a sufficiently broad consensus in support of a system for conducting change.

This must also be the proper task of institutions in international politics: to act not as buttresses of a notionally static order but as the broadly supported mediators of change. Within the international system, they must serve this purpose partly by adjusting to continual changes in the system's membership. Equally, they must be attuned to the changing pattern of the membership's converging and conflicting interests. Our earlier discussion stressed the special importance of the contribution that only institutions can make to sustaining and expressing the consensus on acceptable limits to international behaviour in a changing world. The test of any political institution's utility is whether it can provide a channel in which otherwise chaotically related pressures for change can be induced to flow together in a direction and at a speed that is acceptable to the polity's members and conducive to the common good. A precondition is that those responsible for and affected by change in the system concerned, especially when their interests are naturally at variance, should be disposed to behave towards each other in ways compatible with this concept of dynamic order.

A painstakingly reworked picture of the international system is now beginning to emerge. It will not have escaped notice, however, that the analysis has repeatedly shied away from a notoriously difficult question in any political system: how participants in the system are to determine and adjust the bounds of their consensus. After all, the guidelines for harmonizing rates of change, the norms for testing behaviour, and the criteria for identifying order itself all depend, in one way or another, on being able to identify what the members of the international system will and will not accept. The omission may nevertheless be forgivable, since it would clearly be ridiculous to attempt an instant resolution of what has always been a political crux. However, to the extent that we are concerned with international institutions and organizations, we must make a short foray into this difficult territory, if only to locate one of the many pitfalls it contains.

Politics is the name of the processes by which members of a human society, in their unvarying dual concern for progress and security, bargain about the system of relative values to be adopted by and on behalf of the group when seeking to influence or respond to circumstantial change. It follows that determining what is acceptable in an international system is eminently a political task. In as far as its activities and achievements are necessarily subject to tests of general acceptability by its members, no international organization, therefore, can divorce itself ultimately from politics.

This needs to be said, because one of the well-intentioned demands frequently made today in the name of international order is that certain kinds of functionally expert international organization – the United Nations specialized agencies, for instance – should be purged of politics. It is easily understandable that anyone particularly committed to the aims of such an organization should be eager to escape from the disruption and delay that political disputes can cause. Without question, institutional efforts to pursue long-term international goals of order or welfare can all too quickly be thwarted if those with short-term political preoccupations intervene to impose their selfish or functionally ignorant preferences. Nevertheless, beware! It is no less true that functional dedication within some technically, culturally, or economically specialized field becomes an exercise in ultimate futility if those who engage in it unwittingly or wilfully ignore the evolution of political, and thus societal, attitudes. International order is about consensually controlled change. Forming and expressing the necessary consensus are political activities. International institutions are doubly embroiled: as part of the mechanism for harmonizing and conducting change on the basis of consensus, but also as part of the structure that must itself be subject to constant adaptation under the same rubric. Neither as actors nor as patients can they claim immunity from politics, however seductive the vision of political innocence may be.

To say that international organizations must be able and willing to adapt and be adapted, as well as to play their part in the management of change, is to make an extraordinary demand. There is a strong familial tendency for institutions formed by political decision to cleave to the particular images of order and system that existed in the minds of their founders at their birth. As Kenneth Boulding once observed with typical acuity: 'In every society there seems to be a ceremonial value image which is transmitted by the official and formal institutions of the society.... The image becomes institutionalized in the ceremonial and coercive institutions of society. It acquires thereby a spurious stability. As the world moves on, the image does not.'[5] It is exceedingly difficult to resist this paralytic tendency. With Lewis Carroll's Cheshire cat, it was the body that faded slowly away, leaving only a smile. With international organizations, blended originally of aspiration and institutional structure, a natural resistance to adaptation seems sometimes to reverse this process, so that all else fades with time except the body. It is important, however, that bodies seeking international order should avoid such a trap. A political institution can, in any case, only survive as the tool, rather than the tomb, of its progenitive purpose. At the international level, the purpose of order inevitably has a changing form. International organizations have a vital role to play in the service of this purpose, but it follows that they cannot play it unless they accept change as both their business and their proper fate.

The main reason for regarding formal multilateral organizations as a vital instrument is that, with both conflict and co-operation becoming ever more diversified and functionally esoteric, specialized institutions have a unique capacity to identify and express internationally acceptable norms of behaviour. It is a principal lesson of the last forty years that such norms are increasingly important. Membership of the international system is still growing and becoming more various. The interests engaged are increasingly divergent, as are the rates of technical and societal change that strain the very fabric of the system. In these circumstances, order depends more and more heavily on maintaining a consensus concerning tolerable modes of behaviour. Whether or not their members and managers always recognize the fact, this has become a major responsibility of multilateral organizations, whether global, regional, or functionally specialized. They are, in fact, our available common response to what Boulding has called 'the problem of discovering the appropriate institutions which will guarantee benevolent rather than vicious dynamic processes in international relations.'[6]

This, perhaps, is the real name of international order: 'benevolent rather than vicious dynamic processes.' The unremitting challenge, therefore, is to agree on criteria for distinguishing the benevolent from the vicious; that is, to carry on the perennial business of politics.

It is for this reason that judgement on the question originally posed in my title must finally be reserved. Taking a narrow, conventional, and, I suggest, a profoundly unsatisfactory view of security in the international system, measured only by the incidence of violent conflict, we found much earlier that neither chaos nor order, in their equally conventional guises, seemed likely to prevail. Prolonged elaboration has since, no doubt, enriched the analysis. What it has also done is to expand, at each step, the unfinished agenda and the evident responsibility of politics.

The strains within the international system have increased. Unless their effects are contained, the accelerating but diverging processes of change necessary to human welfare and the human spirit will carry the system inexorably closer to chaos. Against this, there is encouragement to be drawn from the largely unheralded ways in which international behaviour has already been moderated, offsetting that disorderly trend. Carrying the processes of containment and moderation further, however, depends on developing an underlying political consensus. Despite the recent embitterment of East-West relations and the persistent difficulty of North-South relations, I see no reason yet to despair of such political improvement. On the other hand, it cannot safely be assumed. Politics, at the end, remains the daunting challenge, and the response to the challenge continues in sufficient doubt to defeat any confident answer to the original question.

What is certain is that a measure of order can only be preserved by continual and uncommonly skilful effort. I referred earlier to the physical problem of sustaining indefinitely a well-ordered system of human energy use, when every conversion of energy must necessarily tend towards thermodynamic chaos. Some might think that this potentially apocalyptic issue is as nearly intractable in the long run as any confronting us. They would be wrong. Albert Einstein pointed to the truth, in his surprised reply when asked why the human achievement in exploiting nuclear energy had not been matched by success in controlling its use. 'Obviously,' he said, 'politics is more difficult than physics.'

NOTES

1 International Institute for Strategic Studies, *Strategic Survey 1983-1984* (London 1984), 1.

2 *Idem.*

3 Ian Smart, 'The Adopted Image: Assumptions about International Relations,' *International Journal* xxxix, no 2 (Spring 1984), 266.

4 *Ibid.*, 260 f.

5 K. E. Boulding, *The Image: Knowledge in Life and Society* (Ann Arbor 1961), 73, 79.

6 *Ibid.*, 113–14.

JOHN W. HOLMES

3 A Glance at the Record

Although we should bear in mind that the world has been declared in crisis since the United Nations General Assembly first met in January 1946, the present congruence of military and financial threats poses a particularly grim challenge to the formal and informal security structures that have been woven over the past forty years. The International Institute for Strategic Studies has warned that although neither superpower thinks it could gain from a deliberate resort to war 'when tensions between them are high and regional conflicts in which they have opposing interests abound, the risks that dangerous posturing and miscalculation might draw them into direct conflict increase significantly.'[1] This is no time for illusion, but the gravest danger may be despair. Of those hopes on which international institutions were built, one fundamental assumption remains to cling to: that the powers would agree in the ultimate situation to arrest deterioration into nuclear war. This basic commitment still seems to hold in Moscow as well as in Western capitals. Third World countries insist that it is not their problem, but it is only in Tripoli or Teheran that one senses a totally reckless attitude to world order. There is a kind of last-ditch prudence in the actions if not the rhetoric of the

General Assembly and the Security Council and of the great powers. A historical perspective on the changing assumptions about security in the decades after World War II might cast more light on present dilemmas, although this oversimplified interpretation is no more than one way of looking at history, a particularly Canadian way perhaps.

Too many anxious observers, especially senior citizens, persist in regarding the security 'system' set up in 1945 as the ultimate wisdom, a model which has subsequently been betrayed by selfish governments and to which we must return if we are to have peace. It would be wiser to regard it as a brave effort that has at least proved adaptable to the lessons of experience. The system was noble enough, and the creators need not be scorned, but it was flawed by the inevitable determination to prevent wars and depressions like the last ones. For one thing, the classic nature of the German, Italian, and Japanese assaults kept the founders of the United Nations from a more sophisticated view of aggression. The United Nations system was an ingenious effort to build a collective force out of national contributions, but it never got off the ground. Whether the East or the West should be blamed is irrelevant now. The planners had not taken sufficient account of the real global landscape.

The United Nations was based on two concepts which were not entirely compatible. First was the concept of universal collective security, the determination to have in place as a deterrent, in the event of a recurrence of 1939, the kind of allied force that did not come into being until 1941. The second element was more realistic. It was the idea of preserving the wartime alliance as a continuing crusade against further aggressors. At the heart of this was the responsibility placed on the five great powers – the United States, the USSR, Britain, France, and China – to lead in managing an orderly world. The word *veto* does not appear in the United Nations Charter; the role of the great powers was conceived as an obligation to find consensus rather than as a privilege. Smaller powers did not much like this, and they sought with some success to modify the privileges. They accepted the situation, however, because they had learned that pure-in-theory 'democratic' international institutions could not prevent wars or win them. None of the creators was unduly confident that the alliance would hold together, but it was essential to try. Although the idea of 'universal' collective security was already qualified because certain powers had the veto, it was hoped that these powers would give the lead in collective action against misbehaviour.

There is no need to point out the distressing history of great power 'unanimity,' the shift of power from the Soviet Union and three Western powers, and the rise of the third force or forces. Nevertheless, it is worth noting that in the Middle East, where the severest threats of a grand war have originated, tacit limitations have been placed by the great powers on the extent of conflict to be tolerated, and there have been increasing calls for settlements that involve both the superpowers. It is folly, of course, ever to expect too much of the continuing great power management as foreseen in San Francisco, but it would be greater folly to dismiss it entirely. The path has not been all downhill. In the 1950s one would have been considered an incorrigible optimist if one had predicted that East and West would, in the 1960s and after, be in a state of arms negotiation in Geneva, Vienna, and Stockholm – or indeed that war between the East and the West would have been contained into the 1980s without a working system of universal collective security.

Universal collective security as a principle did not survive long. When the challenge came in Korea in 1950 a majority of members, still under the spell of the League of Nations failures over Manchuria and Ethiopia, felt that the United Nations, too, would crumble if it did not respond collectively to this classic case of aggression. It was a near thing, but fortunately United Nations forces were able to re-establish the *status quo ante*. The lesson absorbed, however, was not that universal collective security worked but that it ought not to be risked again. What if aggressors attacked at various places at the same time? The principle could not be formally disavowed, and the rhetoric continued, thereby confusing the public and encouraging cynicism about 'the failed UN.' The organization was useful in the getting of an armistice in Korea – not as an institution for laying down the law but as a site for diplomacy. In the 1950s the shift from the illusion of a tentative world governing body to that of a site for multilateral diplomacy became accepted – in practice, at least. Success in arresting conflict, as over Suez in 1956, strengthened the role of the General Assembly, the Security Council, and the secretary-general in conflict resolution and peaceful settlement.

The peacekeeping role grew out of these two functions and not out of the provisions for collective security, although in the methods of recruiting national contingents there was some echo of the unfulfilled provisions in the Charter for a United Nations force. The 1950s were on the whole a good time for the United Nations in spite of, or perhaps even because of, the tacit abandonment of the illusions of collective security. Aside from the Koreans, most of the forces that were provided for the United Nations in 1950 came from countries that had recently been formed into NATO. The fact that they were led as a fighting force by one superpower was hardly in accordance with the tenets of collective security, but the fact that fighting under a blue and white banner was a grim business, in which military necessity had to take precedence, was brought home to those still engaged in creating an international security system. A military campaign cannot be run by a committee of diplomats in New York.

It can be argued that the United Nations' military success – or avoidance of defeat – in Korea and its comparative success in maintaining peace in the 1950s are both at least partly attributable to the shift from universal collective security to collective defence, a less pretentious approach to peace through alliance. As collective security proved unrealistic, there was the danger of a decline into the kind of helplessness that the 'creators' recalled from the 1930s. The Charter, it must be recalled, was not a pacifist document. It said very little about disarmament, because it believed in armed force in the hands of the righteous (and perhaps also because it was drafted before Hiroshima). Collective security was too logical for this world. The balance of power was a discredited concept; yet the lesson of 1939 was that an imbalance of power could be a greater threat to peace. So those Western countries that were frightened banded together in a collective defence system called the North Atlantic Treaty Organization (NATO), making sure that it was made compatible with the Charter's provisions for collective defence (Article 51). The United Nations would stay universal for conflict resolution and for peaceful settlement.

For some time, and still in the minds of those whose hearts belong in San Francisco, the formation of NATO was seen as a blow to the United Nations. What it did, however, was to pierce an illusion. It relieved the United Nations of a military responsibility that would drag it down. The renewed confidence engendered by the feeling that a drift into insecurity had been arrested was essential so that effective diplomacy could be pursued in the United Nations. It was not easy to see this at the time, but the move towards détente and negotiation was made possible when, by the end of the 1950s, countries from East and West agreed to sit down at Geneva and accept their special responsibility for reducing arms. Although no one said so aloud or explicitly, the Warsaw Treaty Organization (WTO) and NATO became accepted parts of a security system that was compatible with an adjusted role for the Security Council, and a far more realistic one. Of course, it would have been better if neither alliance had been necessary, but both were responses to the Cold War, not the causes of it.

A word might be said about Canadian attitudes on all this. Initially, Canadians tended to be true believers in universal collective security. It was a way of reconciling independence and security. The political leaders, however, misjudged it as a scheme that would relieve them of the necessity of maintaining consequential armed forces. They continued for five critical years to use the unsuccessful efforts to negotiate a United Nations force as an excuse to disarm drastically and remain impotent. They made the same mistake, it should be added, about the obligations of collective defence under NATO. A country that cannot defend itself has a genuinely difficult problem in working out a satisfactory defence policy, and Canadians, during the King era especially, were inclined to rely too much on getting a good formula, with inadequate regard for its credibility. Korea caught them with a wide gap between theory and capability. Although Canada was one of the most loyal members of the United Nations, it had no forces available for Korea and was the last of the significant Western powers to get troops to the spot. At this point rearmament began in Canada, and shortly after forces had been despatched to Asia they were also sent to Europe, an action not hitherto foreseen in peacetime.

Thus equipped, Canada was shortly to provide bodies for peacekeeping within the United Nations and outside it (Indochina). Canadians thereby found a special role that gave the United Nations a new kind of credibility. It also provided a legitimate satisfaction and perhaps an inevitable tendency to exaggerate the capacity of the United Nations. Canada's view of the United Nations as a security institution has been coloured since then by its success or failure in peacekeeping.

The prolonged frustrations of the assignments in Indochina, author-
ized not by the United Nations but by a conference of powers without
continuity, left extreme wariness about peacekeeping outside the
framework of the United Nations. Earlier successes of Canadian diplomacy in the General Assembly and the Security Council strengthened trust in the United Nations as an instrument for keeping the
peace, although in later years they also gave rise to a weary conviction
that neither the United Nations nor Canada was what it had once
been. When Canadian peacekeepers were ejected from Egypt in the
late 1960s and when they were overwhelmed in the sordid war in
Vietnam, the Canadian public said, 'Never again.' Yet, a few years
later, Canadians responded promptly for UNEF II and another round
in Vietnam – partly because it is hard to resist a call to help peace
along when the world is in crisis, and partly because Canada had a
reputation to maintain.

As the role of the great powers in the Security Council became
more consistently paralyzed by the mingling of East-West and North-
South divisions, it was inevitable that the superpowers would act
more often on their own. The United States was a kind of un-
acknowledged surrogate for a United Nations that could not make
up its mind. In the early years, it alone had the economic and military
resources to get the United Nations system launched. Members of
the United Nations could argue over needs and responses, but they
knew that the buck stopped in Washington. Even United Nations
peacekeeping, assigned to lesser powers, was not possible without
United States logistical support. A certain assurance of ultimate security was provided for Westerners and for a good part of the Third
World by the American lead in nuclear capability, or, if one preferred
to look at it that way, by the umbrella of nuclear stalemate between
the two superpowers. The USSR and its associates did not, of course,
accept this American role as surrogate, and they had a blocking capability. Nevertheless, they did not have the power to do anything
of the same kind themselves. American hegemony was largely accepted, though by no means formally or enthusiastically, and only
because a Pax Americana was better than no *pax* at all. In the immediate postwar years, the fear was not that the United States would
use its military power too rudely but that it would again renounce its

role in collective security. Even the Russians in 1945 wanted the United Nations headquarters to be in the United States for that reason.

Inevitably, therefore, the United States acted unilaterally, some-times but by no means always in accordance with its allies. Without the five-power accord for which the Charter hoped, someone was bound to act. What the Americans did was not always serenely wise. They were influenced and sometimes checked by the intervention of their allies and by strong voices from the Third World. It was easier to check them than to make them act. The decision to oppose aggres-sion in Korea was an expression of strong majority will in the United Nations, but only the United States could decide on action, because it alone had the force available. Its role as unchallenged manager of the world and of the United Nations has been considerably exagger-ated both by its antagonists abroad and by its own critics at home. On functional rather than utopian grounds, working arrangements were accepted in which the United States was recognized as more equal than others. So long as the Americans showed some due regard for the opinions of their allies and of the world in general, this was acceptable. Others, especially the allies, complained about American unilateralism, but to a considerable extent they conceded this and even encouraged it, *faute de mieux*. When at times the Americans showed an inclination to avoid involvement – in southern Africa, for example – they were criticized for irresponsibility. Why, it was asked, did they not prevent trouble in Cyprus or East Timor, or enforce human rights in Iran?

This kind of tacit acceptance of United States leadership began to come apart in the 1960s. It was inevitable that Americans would use their hegemony to further their national interests, but in the earlier stages they did seem to act pretty consistently on the principle that their major national interest was a stable world order, albeit one involving perpetual change. The apparent decline of their relative military and economic status has made it harder for a democratic country to integrate the national and the global perspectives. The tragic miscalculation in Indochina undermined confidence in their wisdom. The United States' record in leadership during the postwar decades was more enlightened than one could have expected, but no government can play God in a perpetually godlike way. This is the lesson. The Americans' assumption since 1776 that they are not a nation like others provided inspiration for responsible leadership, but it increasingly made it difficult for them to work towards the transfer of responsibility, even to their allies, let alone to the other great powers in the Security Council. Under an administration which combines an exaggerated concept of the messianic role with an unstable nostalgia for the days of unquestioned hegemony, the problems of creating a healthier multilateralism are acute. Nevertheless, we should remember that until the tragic miscalculation of the Multinational Force (MNF) in Lebanon became apparent, and while American policy in Lebanon still looked reasonably even-handed, Canadians and others were disposed to accept as an unfortunate necessity the virtually single-handed diplomatic effort of the United States in that troubled area.

There is danger in describing in too rosy terms the adjustment from the unrealistic hopes of 1945 to the more functional approach of the era of incipient détente. For a Canadian, the formula of United Nations-NATO and NATO-WTO, as it appeared in the 1960s, was perhaps just too pat. The bilateral world, as we saw it, was an illusion. So is the trite notion of three worlds which beguiles us now. The Third World has some diplomatic clout, but it is not a united force for security purposes and can hardly be said to have any common security interest except the global threats that perturb us all. Since the 1960s, the two superpowers have emerged in the popular view as the only real managers, however much we may dislike this situation. The question now raised is whether this view is valid, whether the superpowers' capacity to manage is declining, or whether perhaps it has always been overrated. A good thing this might be, one would think, provided we have a *pax* of some kind.

The functionalist has a tendency to imply that whatever happened was all for the best, that in any case history cannot be rewritten. A distinction must be made between the descriptive and prescriptive approach. Accepting what has happened rather than wishing it had not happened comes naturally to those who, for professional reasons, are always faced with the question, 'What is to be done?' On the spot, the diplomat must start from the circumstances, regrettable though they may be. The role of the historian, unencumbered by that responsibility, is different. He must expose the might-have-beens so that our structures and strategies may be adapted to the lessons learned.

He is less likely to take the Whiggish approach, which is nevertheless essential for those trying to create better structures. Each approach is valid, provided we know whose spectacles we are wearing.

NOTE

1 International Institute for Strategic Studies, *Strategic Survey 1983–1984*, (London 1984), 10.

4 The United Nations

Introduction

JOHN W. HOLMES

The United Nations was conceived as the basic framework of the postwar security system, but its role has become more ambiguous and much harder to define. It was never assumed that the management of peace had to take place exclusively within its formal sessions. Diplomacy, as usual, would continue in the chanceries of the world, with the United Nations as a kind of reserve authority. However, that diplomacy has been much looser and less disciplined than was expected. There is still a moral authority in United Nations resolutions, but it is maintained with difficulty, partly because the United Nations is so often evaded and its fairness suspect. Still, it is there to be used when a workable consensus can be achieved. Whether or not it is being wise or useful, it is a force that cannot be ignored.

Given the tendency to blame the institution for failure rather than to recognize that conflict in an unruly world is not easily constrained, the first question to be faced is whether the United Nations is dispensable. Even if one thinks that it is ineffectual or that it does more harm than good, can one risk pulling out and leaving it in the hands of what are presumed to be hostile forces? It will not go away and could only be replaced, if at all, by something rather like itself. Secretary-General Javier Pérez de Cuellar has compared it to a Stradivarius violin: 'If you play it badly, or don't play at all, it is not the violin's fault.'

The secretary-general is the ultimate diplomat, whose role in security is too often forgotten. One of the more hopeful signs in recent years has been the dedication and skill of Pérez de Cuellar in using his position to explore and define the kinds of solution or settlement that political leaders of proud states might be prepared to accept. The United Nations is not a world government with power to enforce peace. It is an instrument of multilateral diplomacy – although not just that, for there still is the pledge of good behaviour, which is the Charter. Peace is more likely to be maintained and aggression forestalled by compromise and by the gentle art of saving face than by issuing unacceptable ultimatums, resonantly moral though they may be.

In the present context, the Security Council is, of course, the central body to be examined. Its record of stopping wars is not impressive, and its lack of resolution is more notable than its resolutions. The justification offered is that it reflects, as it must, the realities of a divided world. Here the five great powers and the lesser powers are forced to face those realities in crisis (which they do more frankly in the corridors than in public sessions). The Middle East, for example, may still be tragically unsettled, but the Council can be given some credit for the fact that conflict has not widened into nuclear war. Is this the bedrock reality that still binds the great powers? As one can see from the special responsibilities laid on the great powers by the Charter, it was (regardless of the accompanying rhetoric) conceived as a means of maintaining international equilibrium by manipulation. The effort to define the Council's power in general terms may encourage despair, but the question we shall look at is how to work the levers in actual situations. Some things work; some do not.

Although the founders established the Security Council as the basic instrument for maintaining security, the General Assembly was given its restricted say. Lesser powers, such as Canada, were insistent that the Council, in which the major military powers had special responsibilities, should stick to security and should not set itself up as an executive board for the whole United Nations system. The lesser powers wanted a chance to express in the Assembly their views on conflict situations. With the Council often stalemated and too much controlled by the great powers, the Assembly has, in practice, from the time of the Korean and the Suez crises in the 1950s, quite often been the agency for organizing security. The distinction between the Council's power to 'enforce' and the Assembly's power to 'recommend' has been blurred by the fact that neither can, in practice, enforce. Military sanctions are almost inconceivable, and economic sanctions have not proved effective. Members can only be persuaded, cajoled, bribed, shamed, or bullied into good behaviour. The Western powers (which early on had sought to strengthen the role of the Assembly to counter, when they saw fit, the Soviet veto in the Council) have become wary of an Assembly in which a none too friendly majority often prevails. So they have retreated to safety behind their veto in the Council. The Soviet Union, which had firmly insisted on the undisputed role of the Council in security matters, now encourages the Assembly in actions that are directed against Western interests, while stubbornly insisting on the authority of the Council over such operations as peacekeeping. An Assembly majority, dominated by the Third World, did condemn the invasion of Afghanistan, and Moscow can therefore not regard Assembly support as reliable.

Given the fading distinction between the powers of the two main bodies, and the intertwined role of the secretary-general, it is not wise to look at them in separate compartments. Although a distinction will be maintained, this chapter will consider the security role of the United Nations in its totality. This totality, of course, requires a more extended concept of security than was fully recognized at San Francisco. The importance of social and economic questions was accepted as justifying an Economic and Social Council with the same status as the Security Council, but the extent to which economic conflict would be the main threat to world order has only been revealed during four decades of experience. Now we also hear the term 'environmental security'[1] with ominous implications. Although there is no space here to tackle the economic and social issues as such, they do have to be acknowledged if we are to get a broad view of the security role of the United Nations.

NOTE

1 This novel concept, which had been earlier used in the Department of the Environment, Ottawa, in 1984, was the theme of a conference held in Toronto under the joint sponsorship of the Centre for International Studies and Trinity College.

What Went Right and What Went Wrong? A Canadian Perspective

GABRIEL WARREN

Applying as objective standards as possible, what has gone right and what has gone wrong with the United Nations system? Is Canada doing enough to strengthen the system in practical ways and to encourage others to do so as well?

The first thing that has obviously gone right is that many parts of the United Nations system are continuing to function well even in politically sensitive areas. A few examples may be cited. Most of the United Nations specialized agencies have not allowed political issues to frustrate their vital tasks. The International Civil Aviation Organization (ICAO) in Montreal was able to investigate the Korean Air Lines disaster and to work out ways of preventing such incidents in the future, even though the Soviet veto blocked action by the Security Council. At its Extraordinary Assembly on 10 May 1984, ICAO even managed to amend its basic document, the Chicago Convention, to reaffirm the obligation not to use force to endanger civil aviation. At its recent World Administrative Radio Conference, the International Telecommunication Union (ITU) made a promising start in bringing order to the jungle of high-frequency shortwave broadcasting, a goal which for political reasons has been impossible to achieve for many years. In another politically sensitive area, it has also scheduled conferences to work out procedures for ensuring that all countries will have equitable access to the geostationary satellite orbit to meet their telecommunications needs. In the International Atomic Energy Agency (IAEA), work on nuclear safeguards for the peaceful use of nuclear energy goes forward in a race against time to keep the lid on non-proliferation.

In human rights, the distance still to go cannot obscure the slow but steady progress that has been made, since the approval of the Universal Declaration of Human Rights in 1948, towards the creation of a system of international covenants, commissions, working groups, and procedures which should eventually cover all flagrant violations. States can no longer hide behind the façade of their domestic jurisdiction.

In 1984 the United Nations Development Programme (UNDP) provided $1 billion in technical assistance to developing countries, using parts of the United Nations system as executing agencies. The United Nations Children's Fund (UNICEF) concentrates on the development and humanitarian needs of children. The United Nations High Commissioner for Refugees (UNHCR) and the United Nations Relief and Works Agency for Palestine Refugees in the Near East (UNRWA) co-ordinate humanitarian assistance to refugees.

Under the auspices of the United Nations system, pioneering legal regimes have been established in such crucial fields as trade, law of the sea, outer space, the environment, civil aviation, and telecommunications. As so many areas of international law have moved from general principles into detailed applications, the law-making function has been getting bogged down in East-West and North-South disputes as each pursues its interests. The development of international law is, however, fundamental to the whole multilateral system.

The second thing that has gone right is that the United Nations Charter (like the Bible, the Torah, and the Koran) has proven sufficiently far-sighted and adaptable that the United Nations is still capable of making a significant contribution to peace and security. Experience indicates that there is not much hope for major amendments to the Charter, though I do not believe that they are in fact needed. We have to make the best use of what we've got, and we have to live with the harsh reality of the veto of the five permanent members of the Security Council.

The veto may have blocked the military enforcement action envisaged under Chapter 7 of the Charter, except in the hard-to-repeat case of Korea. It has not, however, prevented the emergence and continuation of the peacekeeping functions of the United Nations under what has euphemistically been referred to as Chapter 6½ (this being located somewhere in the limbo between the peaceful settlement of disputes and enforcement action). Could the 'Uniting for Peace' role of the General Assembly be resurrected to authorize future peacekeeping operations? Probably not without destroying the organization because, from the Western point of view, the Third World majority is not always used responsibly.

The peacekeeping role of the United Nations remains valuable, though it is far from perfect. As the Cyprus example shows, peacemaking has not always gone hand in hand with peacekeeping. The masochistic experience of the Committee of 33, set up by the Assembly in 1965 to consider peacekeeping operations, indicates that some of the permanent members of the Security Council were unwilling to allow the secretary-general and his staff to exercise much discretion in advance of the realities of a crisis situation. Yet when the international community is actually confronted with a crisis, the pieces usually fall into place under the leadership of the secretary-general and on the basis of the operational experience of the Secretariat and individual peacekeeping countries, and with the expertise of international non-governmental agencies such as the International Peace Academy. I derive no satisfaction from the unfortunate experience of the Multinational Force (MNF) in Lebanon. It confirms, however, the wisdom of the Canadian policy that peacekeeping can contribute more effectively to peaceful solutions when it is under the unimpeachably impartial umbrella of the United Nations.

The third thing that has gone right is that we have had five secretaries-general who have managed to fit themselves responsibly to the times. Trygve Lie (1946–53), it is true, had the advantage of presiding over a club influenced predominantly by Western interests. Dag Hammarskjold (1953–61) was the most committed activist; in times of crisis, the international community said, 'Let Dag do it.' As a result, U Thant (1961–71) had to be much more cautious and irreproachably neutral. He had to circumvent Khrushchev's shoe and the obstacle of the abortive 1964 session of the General Assembly with its impasse over the financing of peacekeeping operations. He had to deal with the consequences of the ignominious withdrawal of UNEF I in 1967. During his term, however, the United Nations Force in Cyprus (UNFICYP) was established under the authority of the Security Council, and he did play an important facilitating role of shuttle diplomacy during the Cuban missile crisis. In spite of his extreme caution, Kurt Waldheim (1971–81) did not get reappointed for a third term. It is obviously too soon to draw any conclusions about Javier Pérez de Cuellar, whose five-year term began on 1 January 1982. The times will not permit him the scope or initiative of a Hammarskjold, but he has been responsibly trying to fill the vacuum caused by the unfortunate relationship between the two major superpowers. He has also been trying, with incisive and chilling logic but so far without too much success, to force United Nations member states, in particular the permanent members of the Security Council, to face up to their wider responsibilities. He has not been immobilized by a preoccupation with getting reappointed. One senses from his second annual report, however, that he quickly became frustrated with the lack of progress in redressing the United Nations' gradual decline into marginality in the maintenance of peace and security. Behind the scenes he came close to preventing the Falklands/Malvinas war. He has constantly tried to increase his involvement to bring an end to the Iran-Iraq war, but he has been frustrated by the diametrically opposite positions taken by Iran and Iraq, with neither willing to respond to international pressure. He has used his good offices in many intractable situations (Cyprus, Afghanistan). He is not, however, a magician, nor can he crack the heads of contestants who are unwilling to come to terms.

The secretary-general and the United Nations system which he represents urgently need the 'shot in the arm' that would be provided by a demonstrable success in bringing about peaceful change in one of the world's flashpoints. In Ottawa in 1983, Pérez de Cuellar said he considered that, of all the trouble spots, the prospects in Namibia were most encouraging, albeit still difficult. He took a considerable risk by making a trip to South Africa and skilfully managed to maintain his credibility on both sides. One can expect him to weigh in again at the psychological moment if the implementation of the Security Council's Resolution 435 on Namibia, of 1978, appears to be getting off the tracks.

The first thing that went wrong with the United Nations system is that the Security Council became immobilized by the failure of its five permanent members to face up to their responsibilities. When policemen fight, it is difficult to stop others from doing so too. The framers of the Charter expected the United Nations to play an increasingly important role in guaranteeing collective security, but it has been NATO and the Warsaw Treaty Organization (WTO) that maintain the balance of power.

The framers of the Charter had their feet planted firmly on the ground when they included the veto. Since the USSR and most Western powers had worked together as allies during World War II, it was not anticipated that relations between the superpowers could deteriorate to the point where the United Nations and the Security Council could become of marginal importance. All United Nations member states pay lip service to the need to strengthen the organization, and at the 1982 General Assembly they unanimously adopted a watered-down resolution to this effect; but what has proved elusive is how to move from generalities to practical specifics. In 1983, for example, the members of the Council held a dozen or more private meetings to discuss how to improve the Council's effectiveness. Since most of the feasible ideas would have involved allowing the secretary-general more discretion, the permanent members were cautious, and the exercise appears to have petered out. It is a sad commentary on our times when one is forced to conclude that the most creative person involved in the Council's initiative appears to have been the permanent representative of tiny Malta!

As part of his peace initiative, former Prime Minister Pierre Elliott Trudeau proposed to Secretary-General Pérez de Cuellar that he should organize confidential meetings of the five permanent members of the Council, namely the five nuclear weapon states, perhaps initially to discuss international crisis management and then, conceivably later, to tackle other fundamental problems such as nuclear disarmament. Let us hope that the trendline in East-West relations continues to improve to the point where the participants would agree to meet privately and light a much-needed fire under bilateral negotiations and under the multilateral work in various disarmament fora.

Without wishing to sound too alarmist a note, I keep asking myself whether the member states of the United Nations, and especially the permanent members of the Security Council, will manifest the necessary will to produce results now. Or will they only assume their full responsibilities in the aftermath of some cataclysmic crisis (if remedial action is possible)? There is an unfortunate parallel between developments on the economic/North-South and political sides of the United Nations system. On the economic/North-South side, the major industrial powers have refused to launch any round of global negotiations that could be directed by the General Assembly in such a way as to disrupt the work of the General Agreement on Tariffs and Trade (GATT) and international financial institutions (where the major Western countries have the decisive voice). If it proves impossible to come to a workable consensus on global negotiations, we should perhaps attempt a more pragmatic, issue-oriented approach. Organizations such as the International Monetary Fund (IMF) the GATT and the United Nations Conference on Trade and Development (UNCTAD), with specific mandates within the United Nations system, should be encouraged to get on with their jobs. Otherwise the international community will have to pick up the pieces after, rather than before, the next financial crisis.

It is difficult for the Security Council to function effectively when its permanent members are at loggerheads. What is sobering, however, is the realization that the Council can remain relatively impotent even when the superpowers are not directly in opposition, such as in the case of the current Iran-Iraq war. There are a few members of the international community upon whom it is becoming increasingly difficult to exert pressure to force them to behave responsibly. Although some observers cynically conclude that such states deserve each other, the international community must be guided by more humanitarian considerations.

What is the true attitude of the current United States administration towards the United Nations? While we take it for granted that the USSR's attitude is ambivalent, we really get concerned when some similar ambivalence is displayed by the United States. The United States has stressed that its withdrawal from the United Nations Educational, Scientific, and Cultural Organization (UNESCO) does not represent the first in a series of similar actions that it plans to take against other parts of the United Nations system of which it disapproves. It would be comforting to take this assurance at face value.

In fact, the United States State Department has been reviewing its participation in all United Nations organizations and has an ambivalent attitude towards a number of the most important ones and their activities (for example, the Law of the Sea and its follow-up; UNCTAD; the United Nations Committee on the Peaceful Use of Outer Space; the International Fund for Agricultural Development (IFAD): and the General Assembly's Ad Hoc Committee on the Indian Ocean as a Zone of Peace). The present administration has a very hard-headed view of United States interests. This is understandable and could be a positive, therapeutic force for necessary change. The cure, however, could kill the patient. If the United States were to follow a policy of cutting back on the parts of the system that it dislikes, abandoning in the process many parts that are of special concern to developing countries, this would disrupt the whole system.

The second thing that has gone wrong is that too much valuable time and too many resources are being wasted throughout the United Nations system on extraneous political issues. I am not concerned here so much with the considerable waste in the intentionally political fora of the Security Council and the General Assembly. Often when the Council or the Assembly appears to be ineffective in dealing with a threat to the peace, or when a majority in the Assembly takes a one-sided and impractical position, the discussion can serve as a useful safety valve, allowing time for the forces of moderation to work behind the scenes or even fashioning the germ of a solution. What bothers me is the overpoliticization that is increasingly infecting the technical parts of the United Nations system, which are neither mandated nor equipped to handle such issues. It is naive to expect that a certain number of heated political issues will not be raised, but it becomes debilitating when the political issues begin to frustrate the normal give-and-take between groups in working out consensus on the essential activities of their organization. UNESCO has been the worst offender in recent years and must be brought back into equilibrium.

The most difficult and infectious political issue in recent years has been the attempts of the Arab countries, calling for the solidarity of the non-aligned countries, to expel Israel from a number of United Nations organizations or to deny Israeli credentials for particular conferences. Israel has not yet been expelled from any United Nations organization, but there were close calls at the 1979 and 1982 World

Health assemblies, at the 1982 ITU conference in Nairobi, and at the 1982 IAEA general conference (where Israeli credentials were rejected, leading to a five-month United States withdrawal). Every time the issue comes up, it takes up most of the energy that would otherwise be devoted to productive work. Congress has ruled that if Israel is expelled from any organization, the United States is to walk out of the meeting, withdraw from the organization, and suspend its financial support until Israel is readmitted. This clearly articulated position has helped countries such as Canada to try and oppose (successfully, so far) attempts to expel Israel. Yet the game of 'chicken' continues, with potentially convulsive effects for the whole system.

We take for granted the discipline of Soviet bloc countries on most United Nations votes. It is also not surprising that the developing countries, whether as members of the Group of 77 or the non-aligned movement, have increasingly tried to use their numerical weight to push vital interests. In recent years, this has shown some signs of getting out of hand (such as at a 1983 UNCTAD meeting of the Trade Development Board, where the Group of 77 called the plenary back into session at 2:00 A.M. and, in the absence of Western representatives, forced a contentious issue through). In all of this, some of the more radical countries have been pulling the rest. This has led to the annual repetition of sterile political debates and the scheduling of redundant conferences and meetings, or the creation of marginal political institutions or machinery. However, a new spirit of moderation and realism appeared after India assumed the chairmanship of the non-aligned movement in 1983. This spirit will have to grow to achieve a workable consensus between groups on the most important political and economic issues. A 'paper majority' is clearly meaningless on issues involving power or resources.

In a statement to the Preparatory Committee for the fortieth anniversary of the United Nations, the secretary-general said that he would like to see each member state call upon its best thinkers and prominent citizens conversant with world affairs to undertake a review of the strengths and weaknesses of the United Nations and to propose concrete programs of action in order to strengthen commitment to the aims and purposes of the organization.[1] The trouble with experts, as with bureaucrats, is that they can always give many reasons why any new idea will never work. I trust that on such occasions we shall not set our sights too high, but also not too low; for if Canada does not speak out clearly, and does not 'make some waves,' on the most important international issues – arms control and disarmament, East-West relations, North-South co-operation – then who will?

Some years ago, in September 1983, the Canadian secretary of state for external affairs, Mr Allan MacEachen, proposed a number of practical ideas for making the work of the Security Council more effective. These involved:

– the secretary-general making greater use of his authority, under Article 99, to bring current or potential crisis situations to the attention of the Council;
– informal meetings of the Council to avert potential crises by examining incipient disputes during *in camera* sessions with the secretary-general; and
– additional personnel and resources to increase the secretary-general's 'fact-finding capacity' and for more effective use of his 'good offices' in the resolution of disputes.

These ideas, as uncontroversial as they appear on the surface, seem to have landed with a dull thud. It looks as if we shall have to wait until Canada is re-elected to the Security Council before we shall be in a position to insist from within that these ideas be given a fair try. In what shape will the United Nations system, and the world it represents, be by then?

NOTE

1 United Nations General Assembly. Preparatory Committee for the fortieth anniversary of the United Nations. Draft Report of the Preparatory Committee, 1st meeting, 31 May 1984 (Doc. A/AC 222/7).

The Security Council, 1

LEON GORDENKER

The Security Council represents two contradictory approaches to its principal task of serving as a central organ for maintaining international peace and security. That task, undertaken while the memories of two world wars were fresh in the minds of governmental leaders and the mass of the people everywhere, constituted the single most important reason for the construction of the United Nations.

The first approach to the Security Council envisages a hitherto unknown concentration on making decisions on matters involving peace and security. It sought to create a governing element where there was none or where earlier institutions had proven inadequate. The presumed lessons of the experiment of the League of Nations weighed heavily in this approach and, in part, led some of the statesmen at the Dumbarton Oaks and San Francisco conferences to seek to 'strengthen' the new organization.

The second approach emphasizes the coincidence of national foreign policies and assumes that they usually would be congruent with regard to maintaining peace. Those who preferred this approach to the first generally hoped for the continuation of the victorious alliance of World War II and, implicitly, often relied on an underlying harmony of interests among governments, which were presumed to put the value of peace above that of the strife. If the goals of governments as expressed in their foreign policies indeed fitted together, then the Security Council would need 'strength' only in the event of a rare breakdown caused by aberrant behaviour. Generally, the United Nations, as the Charter proposed, could harmonize interests.

The institutional design that resulted from these rather disparate approaches necessarily comprised certain paradoxical characteristics. The diplomatic art had worked well at both the planning and decisional phases of writing the United Nations Charter and setting up the organization. The United Nations members could accept the product, but this was partly because they could read from the Charter either support for their own emphases or limitations on those of others. In a strict sense, this could be taken as confirmation that national policy, not central governing, took conceptual primacy.

Where the Security Council might be expected to exhibit governing capacities, the legal limitations of the Charter has sharp definition. Chapter 7 of the Charter includes both close procedural and substantive limitations. The application of coercion could take place only after the Security Council made a definite finding that the peace was threatened or breached. This decision could be made only with the concurrence of the great powers, who were supposed to lead the way to the construction of a military force at the disposal of the Council.

Decisions as to the actual use of coercive sanctions, ranging from diplomatic to military, from mild to punishing, were similarly protected. Even with the concurrence of the permanent members, additional votes were required for the adoption of a resolution. Such a resolution could take the form of a recommendation which imposed no legal obligation, although United Nations members had pledged to assist the organization. But the Council did have the power to impose a legal obligation on the members to take coercive action.

However strong such powers may have appeared, they were not to be directed to imposing a solution in a dispute. Rather, sanctions were aimed at arresting violations of the United Nations Charter. Once the immediate breach or threat to the peace was ended, then the Council could seek a peaceful – that is, a negotiated or recommended – solution.

Even peaceful settlement by the Security Council had little of the quality of governmental decision. Nor was the Council a law court; for judicial settlement, the International Court of Justice could handle cases submitted to it. The Council could make recommendations to the parties to a dispute or in a situation that might lead to a threat to peace, but it could not order a solution of anything. Its recommendations, moreover, were subjected to the same national scrutiny that applied to coercion, for the Council could not adopt a recommendation unless the permanent members supported it and unless it had the backing of the requisite majority.

Political tension between the notion of governing and the idea of foreign policy based on national decisions is inherent in the very structure of the Security Council. Aggrieved parties in disputes usually insist that the Council should make firm decisions to end conflict and to repress objectionable actions. Yet the Council, however deep its responsibilities for maintaining world peace, has only the equipment that national governments permit it. This tension endures to the present time, sometimes pulling in one direction, sometimes in the other, but never being absent.

The myth dies hard that the United Nations, and the Security Council in particular, has the task of guaranteeing that no international violence will appear in the world. The organization began and developed on the premise, not always made explicit, that if disputes were taken to a central place for supervision, then peaceful resolution would follow. But the Security Council can neither specify the conditions that promote peace generally nor impose its formula, should it find one, on the chaotic world. Its role has always been as a tribunal of appeal in specific international disputes, rather than as the architect of peace generally. Furthermore, the design of the Council implies that some disputes might continue for a long time without affecting peace and that other disputes might lead to a breakdown that would be followed by coercive action. For those who eagerly hoped that the Security Council would somehow reverse the historical experience that fighting can erupt in the face of good intentions and that it proceeds logically from bad ones, the possibility remained that the activities of the Security Council would actively contribute to a more tranquil world and that enough would be learned in the process to avoid war permanently.

The Security Council has indeed been busy with disputes. It is ready, following the injunction of the United Nations Charter, to come into session at any time. It has been summoned by its own members, by other United Nations members, and, on a few occasions, by the secretary-general. The desks of its members sometimes stagger under piles of trivial documents, submitted by governments seeking free publicity for their views. At other times, the documents contain such material as the texts of U Thant's path-breaking communications during the Cuban missile crisis.

By the end of 1985 the Security Council had met more than 2500 times. Some of its sessions had such *pro forma* purposes as approving a desiccated annual report to the General Assembly; others took up the British onslaught on the Falklands, the American invasion of Grenada, the Soviet intervention in Afghanistan. Some led eventually to substantial coercion, as in Korea in 1950 or the Congo in 1964, while others led to such demonstrations of solidarity as the unanimous denunciation of the Iranian seizure of the United States embassy in 1979.

From the beginning, the Security Council has shown a remarkable reluctance to take items off its agenda. The list now contains more than 130 items, the first dating back to 1946. It includes notations of conspicuous failures, such as the organization of an armed force to be at its disposal. It has not even made a final decision on its rules of procedure, which remain provisional as they were in 1946. Some

items have faded from active memories, such as the armed incidents involving the islands of Quemoy and Matsu off the Chinese coast; others are simply obscure now, such as item 66, 'Complaint by Guinea,' although anyone interested could dig out a sombre letter. Some of the most important incidents, such as the attack in Korea or the breakdown in the Congo, have disappeared from the agenda, because they were shifted to the General Assembly under the celebrated Uniting for Peace resolution, which the United States designed so as to out-flank the results of the veto in the Security Council. Other issues, such as the behaviour of South Africa and the troubles in the eastern Mediterranean, have multiple listings, some of which represent greater attention to keeping a dispute alive than to adding energy to its settlement.

The wraiths of yesteryear's conflicts on the Security Council agenda signify that the institution has failed to govern all the unruly conduct of the states of the world. Even if that had been the intention of the members of the Council, or of the permanent members, or of the United States and the Soviet Union, the Council has nevertheless devoted itself to the management of conflict rather than to governing. It has concentrated its efforts on functions that diplomacy typically essays.

Yet its approaches to conflict have included devices that are of deep interest to those who seek governing capacity. Its experiment with a high level of coercion in the Korean conflict represented a unique attempt to manage enforcement action. In the end, it was frustrated by the return of the Soviet representative to his seat after his fortuitous absence had obviated a certain veto. The Council ex-perimented with considerable skill with peacekeeping forces, those hybrid military-diplomatic corps of soldiers who are instructed not to use their weapons. Two are in place now. It dispatched observers to several parts of the world and gave encouragement to diplomatic negotiations undertaken by international civil servants and by im-partial agents borrowed from national foreign offices. It devolved real authority on the secretary-general to make decisions with substantial political ramifications, even if it always pretended that his role was non-political in character. And it sometimes ducked out of the line of fire by asking the secretary-general to take on negotiations that were unlikely to prove fruitful in the short term, as those now directed to ending the armed conflict between Iran and Iraq.

Adding up the number of pages in the Official Record of the Security Council (which appears in six languages) may buoy the spirit of investors in sources of wood pulp, but it proves little about the Council's success in managing conflict or in reconciling the paradoxical aspects of its nature. Nor does the fact that at times the Security Council has demonstrated some capacity for innovation, or at least for legitimizing innovation, ensure that new techniques will be employed a second time or will become a standard part of diplomatic equipment.

Has the Council managed conflict? The qualitative answer is that sometimes it has, sometimes not, and sometimes somewhat. Recent analytical studies of the handling of disputes by the United Nations, while extending beyond the Security Council, make it clear that the organization has had at least an abating influence in most of the cases it handled during the first thirty-five years. It has usually had some effect in stopping hostilities and in isolating cases. The record of settlement has been less clear. The results achieved by the organization have not improved recently.[1] It can be assumed that the Security Council participated in most of these disputes, even if it did not maintain leadership throughout.

Only one conclusion can be drawn. The Security Council does not reliably manage all the conflict of the world. Furthermore, the creation and operation of regional organizations offer governments multiple devices to employ in their disputes if they want any third-party intervention. The simplification of international relations that was sought in the design of the Security Council has not in fact emerged.

Seeking an explanation for the present status of the Security Council – an instrument that falls short of its expected role and perhaps short of its potential – requires inquiry into a complex set of possible causes. Some will remain necessarily vague and will represent mere intuition.

As an exercise in traditional diplomatic method, adapted to the special institutional setting, the Security Council has done rather well. Diplomacy requires a great deal of contact among the parties to a negotiation and a steady exchange of information. There can be little doubt about the steadiness of the contact, given the number of meetings and their sometimes long duration, and these occasions give rise to unpublicized conversations among diplomats. The conversations and the formal sessions encourage a flow of information, as well as some of the most turgid prose and obvious propaganda ever produced. But this informational aspect of diplomacy, necessary as it is to the management of disputes, leads nowhere without governmental decisions that are favourable to management, and without at least some coincidence of policy. If governments decide in advance that they will have little to do with multilateral attempts to manage conflict, then the Security Council has slight ability to take up the task. Nor can the secretary-general offer leadership or even much salient information if the members of the Council, especially some of the permanent members, oppose it.

An accumulation of evidence suggests that some member governments during the last decade have chosen to give their own foreign policy decisions ever-stronger preference over those tailored to conform to the mode and ethic of the Security Council as an institution. This preference has coloured the performance of the Security Council and has contributed much to its widespread reputation of ineffectuality.

The much-remarked flood of new states, some of them of miniscule proportions in every respect, includes some of the most nationalistic governments in the world. The constant suspicion that their sovereignty is threatened by imperialists, multinational corporations, world markets, secret intelligence services, press reporters, and other assorted malignant influences may also lead to doubts about the Security Council. The extreme case is perhaps Iran, but others, such as Vietnam and Libya, have a similar tendency. The ranks of the suspicious are filled out by governments whose test issues have not been resolved, such as the several governments of Africa which (rightly, I should say) object to the slow progress on independence for Namibia and better protection of human rights in South Africa.

In addition, the tripling of the number of members of the United Nations in four decades suggests that diplomacy, whether in the Security Council or outside it, has taken on a new complexity. Multilateral diplomacy always has involved complicated coalitions, cross-hatched negotiations, and much patience. It has not improved in simplicity by the addition of new members or by the lack of interest in revising procedures in the United Nations or the Security Council. Indeed, in the Council the practice of many governments to request an opportunity to speak, even if they have not been elected to membership and even if the issue is not precisely one of great moment to their security at that time, has only lengthened the proceedings. Complexity deriving from a large number of actors who are to be consulted on any action may encourage governments to act impatiently, especially when they are pressed by powerful domestic opinion.

If on some occasions so many governments are heard that efficiency suffers, there are other occasions when governments do their best to prevent the Council from any examination. Both large and small powers have followed this practice. The Council neither accepted nor sought a role in the Vietnam conflict. The United States has resisted discussion of – and, even more strongly, action on – its policies in Central America. The Somali-Ethiopian war never came into the Council. When the permanent members of the Security Council are involved, they have both the actual use of the veto and the threat of its use as a means of dampening the zeal of the other members. Among many examples of this behaviour is the use of the veto by the Soviet Union in the Afghanistan case and by the United States in the Grenada incident. Incidentally, the United States during recent years has used the argument, once almost the exclusive property of the Soviet Union, that discussion of an unpleasant matter in the Security Council (and in the International Court of Justice) only makes it worse.

Both the South African issue and the Vietnam War illustrate the transmutation of an international dispute into a domestic political controvesy. No African leader, according to current wisdom at United Nations headquarters, can afford to be soft on South Africa; failing much real progress, the African delegates in United Nations bodies seek strong rhetoric, which can duly be reported at home. In the Vietnam War, policy issues increasingly became the stuff of domestic controversy: President Johnson rejected candidacy for another term, and President Nixon made much campaign capital of his plan to reduce American intervention and seek ultimate withdrawal. Indeed, flyers which some United States congressmen have sent to their constituents indicate that they believe voters could be attracted by denouncing the United Nations generally, along the lines sketched out by Mrs Jeane Kirkpatrick, the United States representative at the United

Nations in New York from 1980 to 1985. No doubt analogous politicking goes on in other states. The consequence is that success by the Security Council is judged in the national arena in terms of the degree to which it conforms with the views of domestic groups, not the degree to which it manages conflict and contains its spread.

In addition, the notion of victory in the Security Council, or at least 'strong' representation of a government's views, can be used to promote nationalism. Many of the newer states seek a higher degree of national loyalty. Some well-established governments promote it as a tool of domestic political victory. An extreme emphasis on national aims obviously interferes with the planned role of the Security Council. The great powers, moreover, have politico-military capacities for practising unilateralism at a far lesser cost than would be the case for smaller powers. The United States and the Soviet Union both have long shaped their foreign policies on the basis of national wisdom and have used the United Nations as an instrument. The increasing unilateralism of the United States, so long the leader in developing international institutions and the advocate of international norms, has a particularly sombre effect in the Security Council.

In the more abstract realm of the international system, the existence of nuclear weapons, the widespread distribution of highly destructive non-nuclear weapons, the very large number of actors, the increasing degree of interconnectedness among economies, and the persistent preoccupation of the United States and the Soviet Union with each other's wickedness all affect the operation of the Security Council. The Council has had no effect on arms control or on the several arms races, regional and global, that are now in progress. Also, the gravity of using nuclear weapons and the reliance on them by the superpowers has probably widened the tolerated range of conflict among the lesser fry. The United States and the Soviet Union simply avoid commitments through the Security Council which could conceivably lead up the ordnance ladder to nuclear threats. At the same time, regional powers have weapons with which to pulverize one another without nuclear devices. With so many governments representing so many interests, as well as a widespread scepticism about the quality of international law, the potential for mischief increases along with the complexity of handling it successfully. Finally, distant disputes that once could have been isolated tend to spray poison because of economic integration. This is the case, for instance, with disturbances in the Persian Gulf, because of Western Europe's sensitivity to petroleum supplies.

One possible conclusion from this discussion would hold that the Security Council has outlived its usefulness and is a relic from a simpler time. It is perhaps equally possible to argue that in view of the interrelatedness of states and the dangers of unchecked conflicts, such an instrument as the Security Council provides an indispensable diplomatic facility and that those governments which neglect and weaken it in the short term will pay for their error in the future. In any case, the heavy weight of extraconciliar developments cannot be wished away: it is not the Security Council that will decide on its own future but, rather, national policies set beyond its reach. The Council has certainly not become the governing instrument which some sought; the question now is whether it can continue in the future to manage disputes with even the sometimes meagre success of the past.

NOTE

1 Ernst B. Haas, 'Regime Decay: Conflict Management and International Organizations,' *International Organization* 37, no 2 (Spring 1983), 189–256.

The Security Council, 2

W. H. BARTON

A one-line observation on the theme of the limitations and potential of the Security Council as a security instrument would be that its limitations are serious but that its potential is enormous, if only it could overcome its limitations. The Charter is specific about what the Council is supposed to do: the member nations confer on the Security Council 'primary responsibility for the maintenance of international peace and security.' The Charter then goes on to define the Council's role and the responsibility of the membership at large in terms of the peaceful settlement of disputes, and of action with respect to threats to peace, breaches of the peace, and acts of aggression. Having curt-seyed to principle, the drafters of the Charter then bowed to reality by giving permanent membership and the right of veto to the great powers. That reality, of course, has been reflected in the successes, such as they have been, and the limitations on the effectiveness of the Council, which have been many, in the forty years of its existence.

Over the years, the Security Council can certainly claim to have made important contributions to the maintenance of peace and security, though this is nothing compared to what was promised by the language of the Charter. We thus have to say that because of the limitations imposed by the political constraints influencing the membership of the Council – and, for that matter, the United Nations as a whole – the Security Council has fallen far short of what it might have been.

The drafters of the Charter were perhaps prescient in providing for the great power veto, but they could not have foreseen what amounts to another veto, which has proven to be of equal if not greater significance to the role of the Council: the expansion of the size of the Council from eleven to fifteen members in 1965. This completely changed the structure of the power relationships that had governed the Council during its first twenty years. Seven of the fifteen seats were allocated to the developing regions, Asia, Africa, and Latin America. This meant that provided they could maintain a common position, representatives from these regions would have the power to determine what the Council could and could not do. It is a power they have not hesitated to exercise, and it has had a profound influence on the subsequent business and behaviour of the Council. Perhaps the most important single consequence is that the Council has followed the General Assembly in becoming primarily a forum for the ventilation of Third World concerns, particularly those relating to the Middle East and southern Africa.

In the early days of its existence, the Council gave a great deal of attention to issues that divided the nations of the Western and Soviet blocs. Even though any accommodation reached on such issues usually came about as a consequence of bilateral negotiation, debate in the Council served an ancillary role in making agreement politically feasible. When agreement was not attainable, debate in the Council at least provided a global forum for setting out the issues. In recent years, the partisans in such disputes have become cautious about the use of the Council, either as a backdrop to negotiation or as a forum in which to ventilate their differences, because it exposes the parties to what they regard as interference in any negotiating process that may be going on, and because the reluctance of Third World members of the Council to take sides in such circumstances makes the result of the Council's deliberations uncertain.

There have, of course, been issues like the Korean Air Lines incident, Afghanistan, and the Falkland Islands, which have been of such transcendent importance in the eyes of a large number of governments that the disadvantages of Council discussion have been brushed aside. But it is also possible to list many more which should have been on the agenda but which never appeared, or which were given only cursory attention.

This tendency to ignore issues has been amplified in recent years by the obvious distaste of a number of nations, both developed and developing, to submit themselves to participation in any sort of negotiating process which might interfere with the pursuit of what they perceive as their national interests. It is a sad commentary on the state of respect for the organization and the ideals of the Charter, which are so strongly affirmed by nations on joining the United Nations, that in 1982 the secretary-general felt it necessary to appeal to member nations to consider the consequences of the current tendency to resort to confrontation, violence, and even war in pursuit of what they perceived to be vital interests, claims, or aspirations. It would be nice if the studies instituted by the Security Council as a result of the secretary-general's plea were to lead to an international change of heart, but evidence in support of early prospects for reform is hard to find. The most important single element required is a change in the stance of the United States and the Soviet Union in dealing with each other. This would have a major impact on what goes on in the Council. Even if these two powers continued their tendency to keep issues of East-West importance outside the Council, there would still be enough problems in other parts of the world to give the Council plenty to do and a very useful role to play.

Such a change of heart seems unlikely; on the other hand, it is not unreasonable to postulate that the pressure of events could – indeed, is likely to – lead to situations in which the Council would be called upon to fulfil an important role and in which the value of the United Nations, and of the Security Council in particular, would be proven once again. For example:

1 *The Falkland Islands*. According to all reports, the efforts of Secretary-General Pérez de Cuellar at the time of the war came within an ace of success. The British and Argentinians are now cautiously re-establishing contacts. It would be unreasonable to expect an early resumption of active negotiation to solve the problem, but in the long run some sort of accommodation makes political and economic sense for all concerned. The Security Council might well play a useful role in implementing transition arrangements.

2 *Lebanon*. Over the years, the United Nations has played an essential part in the various agreements and accommodations that have helped to prevent or limit conflict, and it is still represented through the United Nations Truce Supervision Organization (UNTSO), the United Nations Disengagement Observer Force (UNDOF), the United Nations Interim Force in Lebanon (UNIFIL), and the United Nations Relief and Works Agency (UNRWA). The United States policy of attempting to keep the USSR out of any of the negotiations to solve the problems of the area has prevented any consideration of a United Nations role in facilitating the withdrawal of Syrian and Israeli forces from Lebanon; and the French effort to bring the United Nations into Beirut was obviously ill timed. But sooner or later the feuding Lebanese factions are going to come to some sort of *modus vivendi*, and at that point it seems quite possible, indeed likely, that the United Nations will once again be asked for help and might well provide the rationale for the withdrawal of foreign forces.

3 *Palestine*. The problem of Palestine seems as far from solution as ever, and the tensions induced by the impact of current American political developments vis-à-vis Israel make an explosive situation even more dangerous. The past record of Council negotiations to head off conflict is not encouraging. On the other hand, the Council has almost always provided the mechanism to bring hostilities to a halt. Regrettably, it may well be tested in this role once again.

4 *Iran-Iraq*. The refusal of Ayatollah Khomeini to contemplate peace negotiations except on terms unacceptable to the present Iraqi government seems to ordain continued conflict and to rule out the possibility of good offices from a third party to help bring an end to the fighting. But sooner or later a break is bound to come, and since the countries of the region are all perceived as partial to one or the other belligerent, it seems possible that the Security Council may turn out to be the preferred instrument for the development and supervision of whatever peace mechanisms are arrived at.

5 *Namibia*. The Security Council has had a plan, purportedly agreed to by all the parties, to provide for the administration and supervision of arrangements to establish a constitutional government in Namibia. The hold-up has been the insistence of the governments of South Africa and the United States that a precondition for going ahead is the withdrawal of Cuban troops from Angola. One may dispute the relevance of this precondition, and there will always be the question of whether, if it is resolved, South Africa will come up with a new difficulty.

One may draw some encouragement from the above list of possible scenarios for the useful involvement of the Security Council and the peacekeeping apparatus of the United Nations; but even if some of them come off, this does not change the fact that it does not seem remotely likely that the Security Council will fulfil the central role in the maintenance of international peace and security implied by the language of the Charter.

This is not to say that the Council should be dismissed as irrelevant. It suffers from the same problems that bedevil the United Nations as a whole; but with all its shortcomings, the world would be a poorer place without it. It will continue to have value, which will vary from time to time, depending on the current state of stupidity of governments in handling their relations with one another, but mainly as a mechanism – a multilateral cloak, if you will – that can implement, and make respectable and acceptable, solutions to disputes which would otherwise be intolerable to one or other of the parties.

Other values are traditionally acknowledged for the Council and for the United Nations *in toto* as an institution: as a forum to give international expressions of concern to vital issues; as a meeting ground to facilitate direct negotiations between parties in disputes; and, on occasion, as a mechanism for defusing issues (especially of a regional rather than global character) before they boil over. These will also continue to provide a *raison d'être* for the Council's importance as a principal organ of the United Nations.

We should not lose sight of the fact that although the nations of the world may have lost the vision of 1945 (if they ever really had it) and in some ways may have regressed in their acceptance of an international code of conduct, the fact remains that in the course of forty years of attempting to work together through the United Nations, a large body of law and practice has been built up and a complex network of political, economic, and social interrelationships developed, and that these unquestionably affect interstate behaviour, mostly to the benefit of mankind. The Security Council has been an important component of this process and will continue to share in it. In an imperfect world, this is something to be grateful for, even if it falls far short of what might have been.

The Security Council, 3

JOHN W. HOLMES

It is healthier to look for those things that are being done in the United Nations system than to despair over the things that cannot be done – as yet. The prospects are not entirely bleak if one rules out miracles. Much has changed since San Francisco, but in other things we may be recognizing anew the wisdom of the founding fathers; in the area of security, it is easier to see constructive possibilities in the Security Council than in the General Assembly.

There are, as Professor Margaret Doxey[1] suggested, useful things that the Council could do in the way of damage limitation and conflict management. It could propose basic formulae for the settlement of disputes, as in the unanimous Security Council Resolution 242 which set out broad terms for an Arab-Israeli settlement.[2] It could also use its wide powers to identify 'threats to peace' under Article 39 by making authoritative pronouncements, even if those pronouncements were not followed up by sanctions. For example, the United States in 1979 got from the Council an authoritative pronouncement on the seizure of hostages in Teheran;[3] in 1982 Britain went to the Council and got a valuable pronouncement on the Falklands, requesting the Argentinians to withdraw;[4] and in 1983 the Gulf states went to the Council to get a pronouncement on the attacks on Gulf shipping.[5] It cuts more ice to get the Security Council to say that something is wrong than to have the garrulous Assembly, dominated by regional blocs, say so. Such pronouncements would, of course, be even more effective if the Council had a record of consistency. On the whole, there has been an understandable reluctance to move to sanctions, even economic sanctions, because of the unconvincing record of such efforts and the difficulty of avoiding a veto. Third World countries, of course, have been less certain of the ineffectiveness of economic sanctions, but the great powers have to be serious about their imposition. Even in the absence of such commitment, the Third World has seen them as another stick to beat the defaulters. Nevertheless, the Council has an enormous power in reserve which could allow it to do something significant.

What about peacekeeping, one of the few at least partially satisfactory roles the Council has found? No one would seriously suggest that the Council should resume its early efforts to raise a military power against aggression. It should not be discouraged, however, from other experiments in attempting to manipulate forces that might otherwise erupt in conflict. Although there have been times when the Assembly has usurped the function of directing peacekeeping missions, there has been general agreement in recent years that it would be safer to restore this authority to the Council, self-disciplined as it is by vetoes. The General Assembly is more likely to let loose a crusade, with dubious logistics and confused intentions.

So, too, are the great powers when they do not act through the Council. Impatient of United Nations procedures and stalemates, they have been tempted of late to take peacekeeping in their own hands – with dubious success. The precedents set have not strengthened the system. There are, of course, two sides to the perennial question as to whether members should pursue their interests in the Council (or any other United Nations body). Up to a point that is what they are supposed to do, and the health of the United Nations depends on countries feeling that it is an instrument that serves their needs. The question is whether the view is short or long range, and whether they keep ever in mind their national interest in the health of the system, in the perpetuation of certain norms of behaviour.

One may legitimately be concerned about the precedent the United States set by going into Grenada to serve its perceived national interest, without any institutional sanction except the rather trumped-up authorization of a body purporting to represent a few Caribbean countries. The Security Council was totally ignored. Of course, the Security Council could not have been expected to sanction a unilateral intervention, but, given the brutal emergency situation and the uncertain loyalties of Cuba and the Soviet Union, there might have been some blessing for an impartial rescue operation. Certainly, other countries have on occasion acted this way (the invasions of Afghanistan and Cambodia were much more brutal defiances of the Charter), but defiance of the rules by the United States more seriously undermined the restraints on international behaviour precisely because the United States had done so much to promote the rule of law in the international community.

It would have been in everyone's interest if, before the United States and other powers embarked on their unhappy experiment of the so-called Multinational Force (MNF) in Lebanon, more serious consideration had been given to a United Nations peacekeeping force. That headstrong experience has been contrary to the long-range national interests of the United States and the other participants. A United Nations approach could not, of course, have been undertaken without Soviet assent and, possibly, Soviet participation. Furthermore, the Secretariat would have insisted as a precondition that internal sectarian strife be controlled. It may be asked, however, whether there is any possibility of a lasting settlement in the Middle East unless the interests of the nearest great powers are acknowledged and unless there is a return to the fundamental assumption of the Charter about the management of peace by the five great powers.

That United Nations peacekeeping can serve not only a national but what might be called a Western interest has been illustrated by the role of the United Nations Force in Cyprus (UNFICYP), the purpose of which was not just to keep the peace on a small island but to prevent Greece and Turkey from a fight that could shatter the peace in one of the most sensitive areas in the world. One may ask whether it served a Canadian interest to keep troops there at considerable expense for such a long time. Has this not simply allowed the Cypriots to put off a settlement of their conflict? Peacekeeping under the Council does not have a very good image with the public, but even those who have had to cope with its endless frustrations still think that it serves a useful purpose in certain circumstances. Impatience over the UNFICYP was at least partly attributable to the fact that the original assignment of a United Nations force had been accompanied by a United Nations provision for a mediator. As always with peacekeeping forces, the UNFICYP was to be a transitional arrangement while tempers cooled and third parties got to work. It was never the role of the 'peacekeepers' to mediate; theirs but to guarantee tranquillity and restrain butchery while a settlement was arranged. It is the mediation, not the peacekeeping, that has failed. However unsatisfactory the postponement of a settlement, there is value in keeping a conflict from spreading, in limiting if not eliminating violence.

Simply putting off a war can in itself be a good thing if it is not just storing up more serious trouble ahead. It does allow people to live longer, and that is the best mortals can hope for. Peace, perfect peace, is not a practicable earthly aim.

Is a diversion to regional bodies of responsibility for the maintenance of security the best practical alternative to the discredited doctrine of universal collective security through the Security Council? Is this the appropriate deduction from the success of NATO? The logic is not as clear as it might seem. NATO is unique, and it would be hard to find other regions with comparable will, consensus, and resources – except in its way, the Warsaw Treaty Organization (WTO). The will and the consensus may not necessarily be voluntary. There is the basic question of whether regionalism is a process by which certain groupings grow out of necessity to fit particular circumstances wherever they may be, or whether regionalism is seen as a neat and universal system to be imposed on an untidy world in conformity with some utopian concept of world government. NATO and the WTO are certainly examples of the former. Few continents or oceanic regions are comparable. Africa might seem one natural region for a functionally useful grouping. There are obvious advantages for everyone in having the Africans cope with their own security problems, seeking settlements in African terms and keeping them out of Cold War involvement. The Organization for African Unity (oau) started out with high hopes, but it has been paralyzed by its inner contradictions, still willing perhaps but not able to relieve the Security Council of contentious issues or even to provide much help in solving them. There is some evidence for the view that regional bodies, embarrassed by their inability to handle their own issues, are too often anxious to pass them to the Security Council where they can play upon the 'guilt' of the great powers.

Nevertheless, could not those regional bodies that comfortably exist be encouraged to address their attention to actual or incipient conflicts and then report them, if necessary, to the Council? This is, in fact, what the Charter prescribes. According to it, the Council is a last resort after regional and other efforts to settle conflicts have failed. The founders were more practical in their calculation of the amount of conflict the Council could bear than has been assumed. When the Charter was drawn up, however, it was Canada and other lesser powers who opposed leaving enforcement action to regional bodies, because of the fear that security would be imposed by the hegemonial power in the region. The Pan Americans were jealous about preserving the peacekeeping mechanisms they had been developing. But although the Americans regarded their hegemony in their region as benevolent, Eastern Europe could claim the same kind of autonomy. It was therefore determined that any enforcement action proposed by a regional organization must be referred to the Security Council for confirmation. One interesting example of a regional security institution established because of deep continental division, rather than in spite of it, is the Conference on Security and Co-operation in Europe (csce); but since it lacks most of the elements normally found in an international institution, it claims no power to enforce, and although it regards itself as being in tune with United Nations purposes, it is outside the jurisdiction of the United Nations.

On the whole, there seems little dispute with the view that although the role of regional bodies to assist in the process of peacemaking should be constantly explored, it would not be at all good if there were regional bodies and nothing else. It is a historical fact, furthermore, that the decline in authority of the universal Council has not been accompanied by the creation or strengthening of regional bodies, aside from NATO and the WTO. In fact, the body with the strongest roots, the Organization of American States (OAS) has been increasingly fractured and for the most part impotent in coping with conflict in its area. Perhaps it is just an ill-shaped region, seeking to embrace two dissimilar continents on the basis of a now-antiquated concept of the New World.

The successes of the Security Council in the past, in conflict prevention or in the organization of peacekeeping, have owed much to the initiative of a skilful secretary-general. Pérez de Cuellar made some practical proposals in this direction in his first report,[6] but nothing seems to have come of them. What are the implications of what was widely perceived to be the failure of his efforts over the Iranian hostages, the Falklands, and the Iran-Iraq war? Was he perhaps saddled with impossible problems? Yet his efforts did not all result in failure. His role was useful in establishing, for example, the investigation of Iran's alleged use of chemical weapons. Successful action by him depended on the consent of the great powers, and they did not want to strengthen his capacity in ways they might not like. Although the great powers had from time to time praised and supported the secretary-general in particular actions, they had on the whole viewed his authority with anxiety as a potential threat to their domination of the machine. He always had to bear in mind that sooner or later one or other of the powers would turn on him. He could go only so far in being the spokesman of the Assembly majority because, although it had expanded rapidly, there was still a core of rich members who could exercise control over actions, if not necessarily over votes.

Granted that we cannot change the Charter, can nothing at all be done? Must we simply leave things as they are? One answer to this cry of despair is to question the assumption that the only way to 'do something' about the United Nations, or any other institution for that matter, is to produce a new rule, a new committee or commission, or some new gimmick or process. One of the problems of the United Nations might be just this tendency to find agreement on a mechanism instead of reaching agreement on substance. Are there not already far too many useless bodies, projects, and subcommittees of subcommittees absorbing the finances and diverting the attention of a burgeoning Secretariat from the hard issues? Would it not be possible to have a sunset law or a self-liquidating provision when these exercises are set in motion? This phenomenon has done much to discredit the United Nations. Few of these bodies have done much to strengthen the arm of the Security Council. What is most needed is not more tinkering with the institution but bolder and more efficacious diplomacy on the part of all members, including, of course, Canada. One reasonable success, such as that which barely eluded the Council over the Falklands, would do more than anything else to turn things round.

A suggestion has been advanced by Professor Doxey that the Security Council might be renamed simply 'the Council,' because while economic security has become an essential dimension of military security, the Security Council has no jurisdiction in that area. This interesting suggestion would have been firmly rejected by Canada at the beginning because of anxiety not to create a United Nations dominated by great powers that assume the right to act as a kind of cabinet or executive committee for the whole United Nations system. The problem now, however, is not so much to limit the pretensions of the Council as to help it do whatever it can find consensus to do.

While the Council has perhaps been less effective since it has been enlarged, the enlargement was necessary to match in some way the expansion of the Assembly and make it truly representative. Without changing the Charter, there are new practices which might be useful, especially procedures which might enable and encourage the Council to act on its own, as Louis Sohn has suggested.[7] The Council should be able to indicate potentially threatening situations in order to forestall conflict. Could the president of the Council perhaps produce a monthly summary indicating the actions taken during the month? Could there be regional monitoring groups? The problem here is that although the Council certainly has the power, within its existing mandate, to become more effective, the permanent members are satisfied with its toothless condition. They fear that it might bite them if it had teeth.

Even if the Charter cannot be amended, it is certainly true that procedures have been gradually transformed since 1945, and there is no reason why they cannot be further altered in practice. The Coun-

cil's present ways and means were described by Leon Gordenker as
'artifacts of the past.' The emphasis in the Charter was on coercion,
but very little use has been made of Article 36, which empowers the
Council at any stage of a dispute to recommend appropriate procedures or methods of adjustment. The Council's method is now more
a matter of negotiating in such a way that countries can get pay-offs
for compliance. Although the Council was not assigned responsibility
for 'peaceful settlement,' there is a moral link between management
and pressure and the assigned function of coercion. Diplomats can
operate now more on the basis of incentives than of coercion. Although there is room for altered procedures and approaches, the
wisdom of formal codification may be doubted. Nations act in any
way they feel they should in order to achieve their national interest.
In certain circumstances and with certain conditions, they may be
prepared to accept terms, but they are reluctant to surrender their
sovereign right in general terms.

   Given the fact that states cannot be coerced and that they can be
influenced in their behaviour only by very broad agreement, could
there be resolution by consensus in the Council, rather than by voting?
For some years the president of the Council has acted by consensus
on various occasions. After private consultation with the members,
he has produced a view or recommendation without requiring the
members to be counted in a vote. In the interest of compromise,
countries have at times been prepared to accept a position which they
could not formally approve. This procedure has also been useful in
avoiding the veto.

   It is doubtful that the Council could be persuaded to deal with
problems that are likely to arise in the future. W.H. Barton, who has
been president of the Council, has cited his own experience of trying
to promote informal discussions on the state of the world: the Commonwealth countries understood this kind of effort because they were
familiar with the format of Commonwealth conferences at which issues
were fully explored without any commitment to unanimity in the
end; the Latins did not understand it very well but were prepared to
go along with it; the Chinese and Russians would not do so. The
stimulation of informal discussion is certainly one of the important
things to be done, but it would have to be directed to specific issues.

It is not easy for Canada to influence the Council when it is not a member. To an increasing extent in recent years, Canada has exercised the right (as a non-member) to make a statement before the Council, without voting, on matters on which it claimed special interest, such as the shooting down of the Korean air liner, but this has sometimes been done more in response to domestic pressure to take a stand than out of any sober calculation of influencing a decision. It is, of course, a right that is more effective if it is not used too often.

Canada has had a two-year term on the Council about once a decade, which is a pretty good record for a middle power among so many. Should Canada try to get on the Council more often? It seems unlikely that it would be able to do so. The non-permanent seats are customarily allocated to specified regions. Within the regions, membership has to be more or less rotated. As a member of the so-called Western European and Others group (WEO), Canada is about as well placed as could be hoped. Certainly, Canada would do a lot worse if it were assigned to a Western Hemisphere group, with all the Latin Americans. Another opportunity for candidacy will come up in a few years, and Canada should think seriously about whether it should run. As the WEO group has two seats, Canadian candidacy would almost certainly result in election.

However, membership of the Council is not for the faint of heart. Along with the opportunity to protect one's interests, to exert influence, and to do good, there is also the risk of getting into trouble. Votes in the General Assembly or other United Nations bodies may not even be reported or noticed; but on critical issues in the Council, members have to stand up and be counted – sometimes even on television. Acting on principle can alienate allies and customers, and perhaps even provoke terrorist retaliation. It can gravely upset domestic pressure groups. Governments should perhaps not think of such things, but they do. Canada's record of conscientious and independent voting in the Council in its previous terms is better than is sometimes alleged. The record is often distorted by counting votes without taking into account the preliminary diplomacy. Voting alongside Western allies, for example, is by no means an indication of docility. What is labelled as an American resolution has often, in fact, been very considerably amended in order to get the adherence of Canada and other 'supporters.' Such subtleties, however, escape the public and political eye, and hot issues are too often seen in terms of supporting or not supporting our 'friends.'

Whether, in the present economic circumstances, a Canadian government would risk irritating a somewhat intolerant regime in Washington and, more important, whether the Canadian public would want it to, is a matter for serious consideration before taking on the grave moral responsibility of Council membership again. No doubt Canada would find a real sense of responsibility to take its turn, but Canadians should recognize the potential for difficulties before doing so.

NOTES

1 Professor Doxey was the commentator in the session on the Security Council and is the author of *Economic Sanctions and International Enforcement* (London 1981).
2 Resolution 242, adopted unanimously on 22 November 1967, *Official Records of the Security Council, Twenty-Second Year* (New York 1967).
3 Resolution 461, 31 December 1979, *Official Records of the Security Council, Thirty-Fourth Year* (New York 1979), 24–25.
4 Resolution 505, 26 May 1982, *Official Records of the Security Council, Thirty-Seventh Year* (New York 1982), 17.
5 Resolution 540, 31 October 1983, *Official Records of the Security Council, Thirty-Eighth Year* (New York 1983), 6–7.
6 'Report of the Secretary-General on the Work of the Organization,' *Official Records of the General Assembly, Thirty-Seventh Session*, Supplement no 1 (A/37/1) (New York 1982), 2–3.
7 Louis Sohn, 'The Security Council's Role in the Settlement of International Disputes,' *American Journal of International Law* 78 (April 1984), 402–404.

The General Assembly: An Insider's View

MICHAEL KERGIN

Since the United Nations makes its impression on the imagination of mankind through a spectacle presented in an auditorium with confrontations of opposing personages, it may be said to belong to the category of drama. Since the personages, individually or collectively, symbolize mighty forces, since the audience is mankind and the theme the destiny of man, the drama may rightly be called sacred.

CONOR CRUISE O'BRIEN

If, by the term *security instrument*, one means a device to manage crises and to settle disputes peacefully, then one set of criteria must be used to gauge the success of the General Assembly. On the other hand, a different scale must be adopted if one is referring to the larger picture of a system aiming at the development of an international order to promote co-operation, based on predictable and accepted norms of behaviour, recognition of mutual dependence, provision of technical services, and the attainment of highest common denominator standards. This chapter will primarily address the ability of the United Nations General Assembly to deal with specific crises, though the second definition, relating to the maintenance of an ordered relationship between states, will not be forgotten and will be the subject of some comment.

The relevance and utility of the United Nations General Assembly to the peaceful settlement of disputes must, in part, be a function of its constitutional authority. The constitutional powers of the Assembly differ markedly from those of the Security Council. The Charter is clear that the Security Council has 'the primary responsibility for the maintenance of international peace and security' (Article 24). The Security Council is assisted in this responsibility by powers outlined in Chapter 7 of the Charter: determination of the existence of any threat to international peace, breach of the peace, or act of aggression (Article 39); the application of sanctions to give effect to its decisions (Article 41); and the use of military force (Article 42). As an important reminder to member states of their responsibility to co-operate with the Security Council, there is also Article 25: 'The Members of the

United Nations agree to accept and carry out the decisions of the Security Council in accordance with the present Charter.'

The General Assembly, on the other hand, may merely 'consider the general principles of co-operation in the maintenance of international peace and security' (Article 11); 'initiate studies and make recommendations for the purpose of: a. promoting international co-operation in the political field' (Article 13); and, finally, 'recommend measures for the peaceful adjustment of any situation' (Article 14). Thus, in stark contrast to the decision-making and enforcement mandate of the Security Council, the mandate of the General Assembly is deliberative, hortatory, recommendatory, and, God knows, discursive.

The distinction in the relative powers of the Security Council and the General Assembly has not changed, despite the constitutionally significant Resolution 377 A(v) of 1950, known as the Uniting for Peace resolution. Co-sponsored by Canada, it was designed to allow the General Assembly to take action relating to the maintenance of international peace and security after the USSR had vetoed a Security Council resolution that was condemnatory of North Korea. The Uniting for Peace resolution has since been used on only seven occasions: Suez and Hungary in 1956; Lebanon in 1958; the Congo in 1960; Bangladesh in 1971; and Afghanistan and the Middle East in 1980.

While on the surface the resolution seems to transfer the responsibility for collective enforcement action from the Security Council to the General Assembly when the Security Council is deadlocked by a veto from one of its five permanent members, in fact the General Assembly is still constitutionally very much limited in its authority. In the words of Resolution 377 A(v), the General Assembly can only make 'appropriate recommendations to members for collective measures, including in the case of a breach of peace or act of aggression the use of armed force when necessary to maintain or restore international peace or security.' The operative words here are *appropriate recommendations*. This is distinct from the theoretical authority of the Security Council, contained in Article 42, where it is stated that the Council 'may take such action by air, sea, or land forces as may be necessary to maintain or restore international peace and security.' There is no reference here to Article 24.

It is worthwhile to examine the case histories of several incidents that occurred during the 38th General Assembly, in order to assess the Assembly's performance in responding to specific crises. These will be examined with a view to measuring the Assembly's effectiveness in defusing conflicts or in creating a useful framework for settling disputes. One set of issues (the Korean Air Lines disaster and the intervention in Grenada) represents a dramatic incident constituting a perceived violation of Article 2(4) of the Charter, relating to the use of force. The second set (the situation in Central America and in the Middle East) represents ongoing, longstanding, potentially explosive problems. The distinction between these two sets of issues can be described as the difference between industrial or sports accidents on the one hand, and the condition associated with a long, lingering illness on the other.

With both KAL and Grenada, the Security Council was convened quickly to deal with the crisis but was prevented from taking action by a single veto. In each case, following the failure of the Security Council to take action, immediate consideration was given to having the General Assembly (which was in session) take up the matter. In the case of the Korean Air Lines, the decision by the co-sponsors (of which Canada was a prominent member) was that the Assembly should not take up the question as a separate item. This decision was taken for the following reasons:

- The incident was not itself a major threat to international peace and security.
- The issue was currently being discussed in the technical forum of the ICAO in Montreal.
- As had been demonstrated by the split Security Council vote (9 affirmative, 2 negative, 4 abstentions), the large block of 100 non-aligned United Nations members considered the issue to be East-West in nature and would not openly support any General Assembly resolution.

Thus, the co-sponsors decided, for what I believe were excellent reasons, that what was plainly a security question – and one which perhaps most stirred up Canadian indignation in recent years – should not be dealt with in the most visible and universal of United Nations bodies, the General Assembly. Any resolutions would likely have failed to receive even half the vote of the current membership.

In contrast, the co-sponsors of the resolution condemning the United States intervention in Grenada in October decided, once the resolution had been vetoed in the Security Council, to move an identical resolution in the broader General Assembly. The critical difference, of course, was that the co-sponsors correctly judged that there was a significant majority of member states prepared to support the Security Council resolution and that this statement by the significant majority carried considerable weight in terms of international public relations. Unlike the Korean Air Lines resolution, the Grenada text did not single out the transgressing party by name. Its call for action was restricted to the immediate withdrawal of foreign troops and a request for free elections to be organized as rapidly as possible. Its weakness, from a Canadian standpoint, was that it contained some unsubstantiated allegations. The resolution was finally approved by 108 affirmative votes, 9 negative, and 27 abstentions.

A comparison of the two examples demonstrates three essential requirements for a political security question to be treated successfully by the Assembly (i.e., in terms of receiving majority support):
- The issue must be salable, i.e., its presentation must appeal to the majority of member states.
- It must be significant in importance, i.e., have aroused the interest (or indignation) of countries beyond one regional group (KAL's impact was largely limited to Western European and North American states).
- The approach must be negotiable, i.e., the draft on Grenada contained little extreme or polemical language, did not specifically single out the United States for condemnation, and contained some constructive suggestions.

The second type of security question which the Assembly handles is the long-standing, seemingly insoluble problem. The Middle East has been a centrepiece for deliberation since the Assembly's inception, while the situation in Central America was placed on the Assembly's agenda by Nicaragua in 1983.

The perceived threat of the invasion of Nicaragua by other Central American countries and the United States has been the subject of Security Council consideration since the spring of 1983. In September and October, the Sandinista regime was strongly preoccupied with American military activity in Honduras – Exercise Big Pine II, launched in August 1983 – and by increased activity by the CIA-supported contras. Accordingly, Nicaragua regarded high-profile consideration by the General Assembly (as opposed to the more restricted discussion in the Security Council) as a platform to express moral indignation as well as to provide additional insurance if the United States later decided to intervene militarily. Nevertheless, there were strong constitutional reasons for not having the Assembly deal with Central America, and these illustrate its limitations in dealing with security issues. For example, Article 12 of the Charter states that, while the Security Council is exercising its functions in respect to any dispute, the General Assembly will not make any recommendations with regard to that dispute. Furthermore, a widely respected process initiated by the Contadora group[1] had been specifically created at the regional level to deal with the conflict, and, under Article 33 of the Charter, Assembly consideration should only follow a breakdown of regional mechanisms.

When it came time for a resolution, a classical negotiating process was engaged between the Nicaraguans on the one hand and El Salvador and Honduras, plus the United States, on the other, brokered by members of the Contadora group, in particular Mexico. The result was a successful consensus resolution which laid out the framework within which a future process of regional negotiations and settlement could be undertaken. Inevitably, the resolution endorsed the relevant Charter principles, such as the non-use of force and peaceful settlement of disputes, non-intervention and the sovereign equality of states, and the importance of safeguarding human rights. Support was expressed for the Contadora process and condemnation was reserved for (unspecified) outside interference. The various elements of the resolution were carefully balanced: reference to attacks from outside Nicaragua against its strategic installations was offset by condemnation of the continued loss of human life in El Salvador and the destruction of public works. Similarly, reference to the mounting of military operations intended to exert political pressure on the states of the region was countered by a call for democratic, representative and pluralistic systems. The result was the successful laying out of a relevant, balanced prescription for a Central American settlement process adopted by consensus. While not itself resolving the Central American problem, the General Assembly did provide international endorsement of the Contadora process; and this, in terms of moral support and in dissuading individual actions to obtain unilateral advantage, has no doubt had some beneficial effect.

The Middle East situation provides a stark contrast to the relatively successful manner in which the Central American issue was treated. Over the past thirty-five years, more than five hundred Assembly resolutions relating to the Middle East and the Palestinian situation in all aspects have been approved or reaffirmed. Annually, only one or two receive Israeli support, five or six might receive American support, and less than half receive the support of the Western European and Others group.[2] Working from the premise that, in order to have at least the pretence of relevance, Assembly resolutions should have the support of the major protagonists to the dispute (these being, on one side, Israel, the United States, and Western Europe, in that order of importance), there is a kernel of truth to the Israeli allegation that since the halcyon days of the Suez Crisis in 1956, the Assembly has deteriorated into an increasingly irrelevant and rejected player in the Middle East drama. More importantly, perhaps, in its efforts to alienate, isolate and, eventually, expel Israel from the General Assembly, the Arab group has succeeded in contributing significantly to the negative image which the United Nations has among its major taxpayers. The positive side has been to keep the legitimate concerns and grievances of four million Palestinians ever present before the conscience of the international community and to provide the Palestine Liberation Organization (PLO) with a respectable international identity, whose weakening can now only come from fragmentation from within and not from the withholding of international recognition.

A comparison of how the Assembly has handled these two longer-standing issues (whose resolution will inevitably come from the initiation of a process rather than from a one-time imposed decision) demonstrates that success is measured by the degree to which the Assembly can find formulae with which the protagonists will agree. Thus, the constitutionally deliberative forum of the General Assembly rules out the imposition of solutions from the top down. Rather, prescriptions for peaceful settlements must originate with the parties to the dispute, must ripple outward towards their major protectors, and, finally, must be crowned with the impressive imprimatur of the collectivity of 160 member states.

Brief comment should be made on the broader question of the maintenance of international security through an established network of specialized agencies and internationally adhered to principles of law. As is clear in Article 60 of the Charter, responsibility for the discharge of the functions of international economic and social co-operation, as carried out by the Economic and Social Council (ECOSOC), is vested in the General Assembly. Similarly, a functional network of specialized agencies was created after World War II under the authority of the Assembly; and many United Nations multilateral conferences that established international, maritime, aerospace, and environmental legislation, as well as regulating international economic relationships, etc., did so under the authority of the General Assembly. The Assembly contributes, in a very real sense, to the underpinnings of international security by providing a means by which actions between states can be held up for public scrutiny against generally accepted norms of behaviour, by ensuring that certain types of transaction follow along predictable lines, and by pooling and distributing technical information on the basis of availability and need. In this structural sense, relations can be enhanced, understandings developed, and conflicts averted through prophylactic committee discussion and deliberation.

On the other side of the ledger, some of the most serious criticisms levied at the United Nations system in recent years have resulted from the highly visible performance of the General Assembly. Bloc voting, which some observers have viewed as exemplar of the marxist theory of international class warfare, has placed interested and political loyalties well above dispassionate judgement. For the outside observer, tensions appear to be exacerbated by pitched rhetoric and structured conflicts. Frustrated high expectations resulting from simplistically billed and oversold panaceas – global negotiations, the Second Special Session on Disarmament, emergency special sessions on the Middle East, etc. – have devalued the General Assembly currency and have provided ideologically motivated critics such as the Heritage Foundation with an easy and ridiculous target. A cumbersome agenda with more than 140 items, in part made up of redundancies and of obsolete, forgotten items; a welter of overlapping committees, sub-bodies, ad hoc organisms in their thirtieth year; a blizzard of documents, studies, and statements; an allegedly bloated Secretariat, carrying out pointless missions – all these have contributed more to the image of the United Nations as a parasite rather than a pacifier.

In response to those who sketch this unflattering portrait, one asks, 'What national parliament is not a government by bloc voting in which the rhetoric of debate differs from the reality of private dialogue and commerce?' Congresses and parliaments produce millions of words, spawn countless committees and cumbersome fact-finding missions, and often deal with parochial issues. But their existence and vocalism assist the process of democracy which, I think, we all believe is a fundamental element in maintaining security. From this perspective, it may be easier to view the United Nations General Assembly as an instrument which, in this general and philosophical sense, does indeed contribute to the maintenance of international peace and security.

In closing, it is perhaps apt to quote from Abba Eban, former Israeli foreign minister: 'With all its imperfections, the United Nations system is still the only incarnation of a global spirit. It alone seeks to present a vision of mankind in its organic unity. There was never a time in human history when so many people cross their own frontiers and come into contact with people of other faiths and nationalities. Parochialism is becoming slowly eroded by the new accessibility. The dynamic of sovereignty is such that it resists all attempts to weaken it, but the compulsions of survival are bound to assert themselves in favour of new forms of integration.'[3]

Despite its fractiousness, the United Nations General Assembly provides important mechanisms which facilitate the process of integration, and thus it ultimately enhances the prospects for international stability.

NOTES

1 The Contadora group originated in a meeting of the foreign ministers of Columbia, Mexico, Panama, and Venezuela on the Isla de Contadora in January 1983.
2 The Western European and Others group was so designated as the mechanism to select two representatives at a time to be non-permanent members of the Security Council. It includes Canada, Australia, and New Zealand.
3 Abba Eban, The New Diplomacy: International Affairs in the Nuclear Age (New York 1983).

The General Assembly

JOHN W. HOLMES

In the eyes of most people, and especially the severe critics, the General Assembly is 'the United Nations.' Its deliberations in New York get little enough attention, but they get a good deal more than the lower-keyed agencies and commissions in Geneva, Vienna, or elsewhere, whose work is more credibly constructive. For the media, the main interest is in the clash and the confrontation. One cannot, however, blame the media for the behaviour of the members of the General Assembly, which has by no means always been edifying.

Contrary to the impression often given by commentators, the Assembly is not and never was intended to be a legislature capable of passing binding legislation for the world or of levying payments that had to be forthcoming like national taxes. Critics like to imply this kind of menace in the hands of a hostile and united bloc of the Third World, but too many professed supporters of the United Nations confirm this impression by assuming that the Assembly should command and should be obeyed in all things. It is the misguided imposition of the norms of national government on an association of sovereign states. On Assembly resolutions, Western and other members have always accepted or rejected or abstained, as their interests or consciences dictated, whether the resolutions called for financial subscriptions to favoured causes or for pronouncements on racism, colonialism, totalitarianism, or other forms of perceived misbehaviour by one country or another. Nevertheless, pronouncements by a majority or by significant states cannot be too casually disregarded without weakening the fabric. They must carry some moral authority and be rejected with reluctance and with good cause. There is no doubt that the resolutions and the rhetoric of Third World representatives in the Assembly in the past decade or more have seriously affected the respect in which the United Nations is held. Whether the damage is attributable to the failure of objectivity on the part of the developing countries or the disregard of their wishes by the West and the hypocritical support, in words but not deeds, by the Soviet bloc is a fair subject for debate, but not for simple answers.

The use of its bloc majority by the Third World (which includes countries as diverse in their deserving of sympathy as Chad and Argentina) is habitually justified on the grounds that the United States, or the West, controlled the United Nations in earlier days and that it is now the turn of others. This raises, of course, the question as to whether two wrongs make a right. It also ignores, to some extent, the curious fact that while the organization was supposedly controlled by the capitalist West, the Third World acquired its new power, and the economic and social programs of the United Nations were diverted almost entirely to the aid of developing countries.

It might also be recalled that it was the 1955 revolt of the lesser powers, led by Canada, that broke through the resistance of the great powers to expanded membership and opened the way for the flood of new and mostly poor countries. The extent to which the United States or the West actually controlled rather than dominated the United Nations has been considerably exaggerated. From the beginning, the voice of such powers as India was very strong in the Assembly.

Nevertheless, the Third World's use of its newfound power, arbitrary as it may often seem, has some justification as a corrective, and it has produced results for Third World countries by its enlargement of the Assembly's agenda. The confrontation is by no means as simple as is implied. There are many kinds of Third World government, left, right, and centre, including powerful influences, usually behind the scenes, arguing that the passing of strident resolutions and intransigent alignment on Middle East questions, for example, are of little value if they are consistently ignored by the powerful. The developed countries also vary in their approach to North-South issues, from the hard line of the present United States and United Kingdom governments to the more conciliatory stance of the Scandinavians, Dutch, Australians, and Canadians. The Assembly's purported function as a forum for letting off steam, for warning of conflict ahead, and sometimes for conciliation is by no means dead, although the sound and fury as reported does not encourage undue optimism. There is, however, a real question as to whether angry debate encourages conciliation or confrontation, and whether the Assembly does more harm than good to the cause of peace. Whatever one's view, the Assembly exists as a fact of international life and cannot be exorcized.

Expectations of the role that the Assembly could currently play in the maintenance of security are, to say the least, restrained. True, in a time of détente, the Assembly of 1978 worked out a remarkable course on disarmament, founded on a broadly based consensus. By 1983, however, the various groups were talking past one another. The Russians were making cynical use of the First Committee, which dealt exclusively with disarmament, by supporting Third World resolutions in order to curry favour – but without any serious intention of acting in the spirit of the resolutions. The Americans were certainly not doing their best, though at least they were more honest about the wording of the resolutions they were prepared to accept. In spite of everything, a dialogue was being maintained among the diplomats, even if this was not apparent in open sessions. Although the Assembly was not being very useful on arms control, this did not mean that it was irrelevant.

The Assembly's capacity to deal with arms control and disarmament is one criterion by which to judge its role in security. Professor Rod Byers of York University, an adviser to the Canadian delegation at the 38th General Assembly in 1983, has noted that the First Committee, being a committee of the whole, inevitably reflected the international debate between the United States and the USSR, with inputs from the non-aligned. Given that East-West relations were in disarray and that no meaningful dialogue had at that time been taking place between the superpowers, it was thus not surprising that the major powers were urged to address more seriously the range of issues under negotiation in the various arms control and disarmament fora. These discussions had produced no meaningful results during the early 1980s, and the Assembly's debate reflected the lack of consensus, with 'an added touch of chaos' from the contributions of the non-aligned. The trend towards a greater number of resolutions continued. The committee considered more than seventy-five resolutions on arms control and disarmament, as well as a number dealing with other international security issues. All of these had to be debated, reviewed, and voted on between mid-October and mid-December. Needless to say, this raised difficult timetable and scheduling problems. The chairman resolved the procedural dilemma by dividing the resolutions into fourteen clusters, having in mind that there were some that could be agreed on by consensus. During the early stages of the debate, consensus did in fact emerge on some twenty resolutions relating primarily to issues which were not central to current concerns; in which the major powers and the non-aligned had no vested interests; in which no current or future weapons developments were involved; and in which no competing or overlapping resolutions had been tabled. These were for the most part follow-up measures to the Second Special Session on Disarmament (UNSSOD II) of 1982, confidence-building measures, issues concerning the seabed/ocean floor, and some measures on the process of disarmament within the framework of the United Nations.

The only substantive cluster in which consensus emerged dealt with chemical and biological warfare. Here, competing resolutions had been introduced – East, West, and non-aligned. Agreement was reached largely because the United States modified its position. According to some reports, however, United States support was related to the Reagan administration's wish to use its stand as leverage to gain support for the congressional funding of new American chemical warfare capabilities.

No consensus emerged on other substantive issues. These included such important matters as the Intermediate Nuclear Force (INF) negotiations, the relation of nuclear weapons to nuclear war, tests (including a comprehensive test ban), a nuclear freeze, negative security guarantees, nuclear weapon-free zones, the military use of outer space, military budgets, and naval limitations. There was, moreover, no agreement on resolutions concerning disarmament mechanisms and review committees within the framework of the United Nations. In nearly all these cases competing resolutions were introduced, usually one each from the West, the East, and the non-aligned. In most cases voting was along these lines, with the non-aligned supporting resolutions from all three sources. As a result, all the resolutions voted on in the First Committee received majority support in the plenaries, even though many of them seriously overlapped each other.

In general, the Soviet Union and its allies were able to vote with a majority of the non-aligned more often than the United States or the West were. The Soviet bloc supported more than three-quarters of those resolutions on which votes were recorded, as compared with less than a quarter which won United States support. Canadian voting reflected the extent to which Western nations in general (with the exception of Britain, which tended to follow the United States pattern) were able to support the resolutions – about 40 per cent. A comparison of the voting of Canada and Romania, the somewhat undisciplined Soviet ally, is interesting. Whereas the USSR and Romania were together on 75 per cent of the resolutions, Canada and the United States voted the same way on 60 per cent. Nevertheless, on the key issues there was a high degree of consensus within both blocs.

An indication of the Soviet view of the First Committee came from an interview which Professor Byers had with a member of the Soviet delegation. The work of the First Committee, the Russian said, was not all that significant, but the trend in voting had favoured the Soviet Union and this was of some importance – especially in public relations with the Third World. In the absence of any progress in arms control, however, he thought it was difficult to be optimistic about the First Committee. He would prefer to see meaningful negotiation on arms control. On balance, Byers thought that the Russians did not expect the First Committee to do anything meaningful, though they appeared to take its activities more seriously than the United States did.

The Americans realized that they had become increasingly isolated in the committee, but their attitude was 'So what?' They gave the impression that the debate was something to be endured. They had little time for the process and attached no significance to its work. This seemed in keeping with the attitude of the Reagan administration on the role of the United Nations in general, and more particularly with that of United States Ambassador Jeane Kirkpatrick. One exception to this attitude concerned the maintenance of consensus within the West and in NATO, especially on key issues. This was particularly true over the issue of INF. There was evidence here, and in the so-called Barton Group,[1] of the view of Richard Burt of the State Department that the major function of American NATO policy was 'alliance management.' In general, the allies were able to maintain consensus on key issues, but the strain showed. The outer space resolution, for example, posed a dilemma for NATO members. Canada, with the majority in NATO, sought, unsuccessfully, to get United States agreement on arms control in outer space.

Professor Byers concluded that from all appearances, and according to many observers, the General Assembly was becoming less and less relevant on issues of international security, arms control, and disarmament, and that it offered little in the way of guidance to the international community on these issues. The work of the Assembly was viable only when agreement existed between the superpowers and when East-West relations were being pursued with some degree of normality. Thus, when the United Nations was most needed, it was least effective. This was the unfortunate consequence of national attitudes being projected into the deliberations. Without leadership from the major powers, particularly the superpowers, there was an absence of political will to reach real arms control accords. In the words of one Canadian delegate to the 38th Assembly, the work of the First Committee had proved that 'disarmament is a growth industry without a future.'

Robert Reford, who had watched the United Nations closely from its early days, when he was a correspondent assigned to it, until his recent experience as an adviser to the UNSSOD II in 1982, has presented a somewhat different perspective. He has drawn attention to the many contributions made to the United Nations by Third World countries and by some of their very able representatives on delegations and in the Secretariat. Disappointment with the United Nations as an instrument for international security is confined primarily to the Western countries, especially the United States, for Third World countries continue to take the United Nations very seriously. Dag Hammarskjold recognized this a quarter of a century ago when, in his confrontation with Khrushchev at the 1960 session, he said: 'It is not the Soviet Union or, indeed, any other big power who need the United Nations for their protection; it is all the others. In this sense the organization is first of all *their* organization, and I deeply believe in the wisdom with which they will be able to use it and guide it.'

Why does the Third World pay such attention to the United Nations? Reford has suggested that one reason is the relatively ineffective performance of regional organizations and the absence of any such organization for Asia. The United Nations, he points out, is the one place where developing countries are, in a sense, on an equal footing with the great powers and where they are able to have considerable control over the agenda. Many of them send their best-qualified people to the United Nations. This mission is regarded as a better appointment than ambassador to Washington. These talented men and women have made important contributions to the organization's work over the years. It was Malta's proposal about the seabed being the common heritage of mankind which set off the great exercise of determining a universal law of the sea. The representatives from the Third World have been effective not only in pressing their own interests but also in the effort to find compromise.

What about the other players in the Assembly? The USSR, habitually on the defensive, has never been a really constructive force. However, the United States has. This has made the performance of the Reagan administration particularly regrettable. Not only the members of the United States administration but even old hands in the professional service have recently shown no interest in the Assembly.

The Assembly's problem, which has become more acute with the expanded membership, has always been how to get enough agreement for constructive action, rather than descending to denunciation and the concoction of fruitless propositions. Members of the Assembly now need to get used to the new equilibrium and seek a new consensus. This fact of life has not been recognized by the men in power in Washington. They have reflected, all too well, negative American attitudes to international institutions, a position summed up as: 'We are a world power. We have the money. You play it our way or forget it.' The typical case was the withdrawal from UNESCO, which has raised the distinct prospect of the United States walking out of more agencies.

What can Canada do in the present situation? Professor Byers is critical of the Canadian performance. He has noted a lack of strong leadership at the political level, the absence of a full-time ambassador for disarmament,[2] and a lack of professional expertise in these complex issues on the political level, at the Permanent Mission and in Ottawa. He has also observed that the Canadian delegation appears to accept the view that 'alliance management' is the order of the day and that the emphasis has been on retaining solidarity with the Barton Group rather than on attempting to reach broader consensus in the First Committee; the delegation appeared to be more concerned in voting on the outer space resolution in the light of American reservations than in making its position consistent with that of Prime Minister Trudeau in his peace initiative. Nevertheless, Byers has concluded that in view of the fact that Canada, like the other allies, has to be aware of the prevailing moods in Washington and Moscow, it is not likely that more active Canadian initiatives would produce more meaningful results. Yet this estimate may do less than justice to the Canadian role. Robert Reford has noted that the members of the Canadian delegation sought strenuously in the 1982 UNSSOD to see how the prime minister's several initiatives might be promoted in the arms control discussions, using their good contacts with all camps and engaging in constant diplomatic negotiation. It was in this way, rather than by spectacular initiatives on their own, that real progress might be made. Their most useful role was in strengthening or modifying what was on the table.

However, the Assembly is not a negotiating body, whether on arms control or on North-South issues. It is the forum for airing diverse opinions, for setting the agenda and urging on the negotiators, who meet for the most part in Geneva. One cannot judge Canadian zeal just by what is done in this kind of debate. It may be more important to deploy the available experts in the negotiating bodies, such as the Disarmament Commission or the Stockholm Conference on Confidence- and Security-Building Measures and Disarmament in Europe (CCSBMDE), where some progress might be made. The political leaders are more valuably engaged at the Assembly, because there arms control is a political issue. Political leaders are not likely to be specialists, and since arms control negotiations have become an area of intense specialization, the professionals are needed for negotiation with their peers. While one may argue that there ought to be many more specialists in the foreign service and that recent efforts to increase their number have not been satisfactory, one should remember that extensive support was provided for Prime Minister Trudeau's initiative. Moreover, a considerable program was set up for the study of means of verification, as a Canadian contribution to the cause. The Department of External Affairs' disarmament fund was doubled to $350,000 for the 1984-85 financial year, and a large sum was set aside for the new Ottawa-based Canadian Institute for International Peace and Security. Canadian efforts should, for the time being, be directed towards what has been called 'damage limitation.' Canada should try to influence the regime in Washington in whatever ways are possible, seeking like-minded countries to work with it in this endeavour. (This is known as 'the herd instinct' in diplomacy.)

As an indication that Canada could exercise this kind of influence effectively, there is the example of the Barton Group. This is an informal body comprised of representatives who are roughly from the OECD countries and who meet more or less regularly to consider ways and means of making progress on disarmament and arms control. It was established in the 1970s, largely under the influence of W.H. Barton, who at the time was Canada's ambassador and permanent representative to the United Nations in New York, and it has continued to meet ever since at the Canadian Mission. It has operated not as a bloc to co-ordinate policies but as a forum for the exchange of views on substantive issues. Nor is it a caucus of NATO members. Its aim has been not just to advance Western interests or to strengthen confrontation but to seek out ways of making progress with the Russians or the Third World powers. This kind of group diplomacy is the only way in which to create movement in an otherwise anarchical Assembly.

A consequence of working with groups of this kind is that Canada, along the way, has always had to sacrifice a certain amount of independence. Although there is no formal obligation for such a group to speak with a single voice, there is inevitably a certain amount of give and take in the normal course of working with others towards a desirable position. This has quite often meant supporting a position without being in total agreement. It is worth noting that the kind of serene independence which some Canadians seem to demand of their representatives in international diplomacy would amount to the strength of a eunuch.

There is not very much fresh or hopeful that one can say just now about the Assembly, except perhaps to cling to the recollection of the consensus achieved in 1978 in the blessed regime of détente. If the Assembly reflects the state of international relations and continues to do so, then its powers could revive if and when the current era of high tension passes. It should be recognized that it is not only the Western powers that feel frustrated. The Russians may see some advantage in hitching their wagon to the Third World's star, but their role is less and less appreciated by those who use their support for their own ends but keep them at arm's length. Even though the communist powers will vote for Third World resolutions on peace and disarmament, these resolutions are in intention directed against both camps. In the eyes of the developing countries, the East Europeans are part of the industrialized world, and the Russians have as much as the West to fear about a 'new international economic order.' The Third World is winning only pyrrhic victories in the Assembly, and the result is that the powerful countries are acting more and more through other bodies. Some new vitality is more likely to come from a state of mutual frustration than from the triumph of one side or another.

NOTES

1 On the Barton Group, see p. 96 below.
2 Professor Byers was referring to the fact that J. Alan Beesley of the Department of External Affairs left the post in August 1983. Since September 1984 it has been filled by Douglas Roche.

5 NATO and Western Security

Introduction

JOHN W. HOLMES

In the public mind, the North Atlantic Treaty Organization (NATO) and the United Nations are still often regarded as antithetical. There are advocates of a strong NATO and advocates of a strong United Nations, and they tend to deplore each other. NATO, however, was conceived as a necessary complement to an overextended United Nations system. It can be assumed, without necessarily saying so, that the Warsaw Treaty Organization (WTO) is also a legitimate response to the same felt need. In the 1970s these two adversarial associations established a *modus vivendi* in the interests of détente. The logical consequence of the changing concept was the Conference on Security and Co-operation in Europe (CSCE), which brought the states of East and West together and included the European neutrals and non-aligned.[1]

Whether it is to be deplored or not, NATO is a fact and will almost certainly continue to be a major factor in security, whether or not Canada is a member. It is wise to bear in mind, however, that it was originally established as a regrettable necessity and that its eventual withering away, along with the WTO, may be a legitimate if somewhat distant aim. Or should these two security structures, having come to terms with each other, be regarded as permanent fixtures in a new fabric of peace and security – at least for a transitional phase?

The bringing together of the states of East and West in the CSCE raises the question whether the future might lie in diverting more authority to regional or functional bodies. Popular perceptions would probably regard NATO as having been more successful than the United Nations in contributing to Canada's security. However, one must first ask whether NATO is really a regional body. Its founders deliberately justified it not as a regional body under Article 53 of the United Nations Charter but in accordance with Article 51, which permits combined action in self-defence. It is doubtful if an alliance that stretches from western Turkey to Alaska is truly regional, and in fact it was originally conceived as an association of those members of the United Nations who were prepared to do something about collective defence.

Avoiding the regional classification was important in view of the Charter's prescription that regional security bodies must report to the Security Council (Article 54). That would have enabled the Russians to poke their noses into NATO business and use their veto. Even if NATO is unique, there still remains the possibility that other kinds of grouping might play useful roles in settling conflicts and maintaining order. Our discussion of this possibility in Chapter 4 rather discounted the expectations for regionalization of the functions of the Security Council. Given the disenchantment with universality, however, it is hard to know where else to look. Is the only alternative a very tense condominium of the superpowers?

Within NATO itself there is, of course, some regional devolution. The regional commands in Europe are, except for the French, under central command. The provisions for North American defence have a more ambivalent status. There is a popular misconception that North American Aerospace Defence (NORAD) is a bilateral alliance between Canada and the United States, somehow parallel with NATO. However, NORAD is not an alliance. The alliance between the two countries is NATO. The principle of defence co-operation in the northern part of the continent was established in the 1940s. NORAD, which was not created until 1957, is simply an arrangement for co-operative aerospace defence if the continent is attacked. Contrary to the wishes of many Canadians, NORAD was not made a specific command of NATO, because the Americans wanted no European interference in the defence of North America, and the Europeans had no wish to be involved. Nevertheless, it has been made clear in Canadian official pronouncements that this arrangement for the defence of Canada's northern region is regarded as an administrative provision within the NATO context. Although the NORAD agreement calls for consultation between the United States and Canada on broad strategic issues, it is not itself an instrument of consultation like NATO. This function is carried on in the Canada–United States Permanent Joint Board on Defence, a consultative and advisory body which was established in 1940.

Although the mechanisms for North American defence are bilateral, both countries have regarded their continental strategies as, of necessity, being complementary to their NATO requirements. 'Fortress America' may always be a fall-back position. The threat of American isolationism – and the even more modest threat of Canadian isolationism – is always a factor for calculation, but it is certainly not the preferred position of either government. The rational deployment of forces is, however, a constant preoccupation, especially in Canada. Canada has always insisted that NATO is a two-continent alliance and that therefore any movement of Canadian forces from Europe to Canada is not necessarily to be regarded as a 'withdrawal' from NATO. Nevertheless, the fact that it would be widely regarded as a withdrawal, unless it was in accordance with a strategic plan agreed to by the Alliance, is an unavoidable aspect of Canadian policy-making.

The strategic problems of continental defence and the whole of NATO are too complex for detailed consideration in this volume, which in any case is concerned not so much with strategy as with structures: with the broad shape of NATO, with Alliance consultation, with the relation of the European allies to the United States and the relation of Canada to both, with responsibilities outside the NATO area, and with the inescapable quandaries about Washington's intentions and the allies' part in grand strategy.

The success of NATO as a consultative body has always been a matter of primary concern to Canada. At the beginning it was assumed that countries which might be required to fight together should concert their diplomacy. For this there was established the NATO Council and the meetings of foreign ministers. Canada insisted, in addition, that there should be mutual respect for each other's economic interests, that an alliance could not hold fast in peacetime if its members were conducting economic warfare against one another. This was the true meaning of Article II, which Canada pressed, and on the whole it has been taken more seriously than is usually recognized. Economic competition among the allies is not unbridled. Canada, too, has seen NATO as the one forum in which it could hope to influence United States defence policies and Alliance strategy. This was a major advantage of a multilateral alliance in which smaller countries could combine for greater weight.

The concern about consultation is not one that will ever be settled. Formulas that actually work are perpetually elusive. Of late, questions for Canadians have been provoked by two trends. In the first place, there has been the straining of the European members towards common policies and the consequent threat of the isolation of Canada. In the second place, there is the apparent disposition of the Reagan administration to act unilaterally and to expect loyalty rather than the sharing of decision-making. Whereas, after Vietnam, President Richard Nixon and Secretary of State Henry Kissinger were looking at ways of sharing responsibilities, recognizing that the United States could no longer aspire to being the world's policeman as well as its banker, the new Republicans seem to prefer the imperial way, with considerably less concern than in the past for the views of their allies.

NOTE

1 See Robert Spencer, ed., *Canada and the Conference on Security and Cooperation in Europe* (Toronto, 1984).

The State of the Alliance

ROBERT CAMERON

On 31 May 1984, in Washington, where the North Atlantic Treaty had originally been signed, the North Atlantic Alliance celebrated its thirty-fifth birthday. Approaching middle age, it has shown remarkable resilience in confronting the internal stresses generated by periodic crises. As more than one observer has commented, the history of the Alliance is a history of crises. In the mid-1980s it is again experiencing a period of considerable strain. While differences are to be expected, given the different types of government among its members and the differing national interests and priorities, what is unusual and potentially more serious about the present situation is that member countries appear to be losing the traditional sense of the overwhelming importance of Atlantic security and seem to be unwilling ultimately to submerge their differences in a common cause. This point was made in *Canada and Western Security*,[1] whose authors believe that in its struggle to preserve its unity, the Alliance has neared a danger point.

Similar concern has been voiced elsewhere on both sides of the Atlantic. Writing in the influential West German weekly newspaper *Die Zeit*, Christoph Bertram, the paper's chief political editor, observed that the debate over deployment of medium-range nuclear missiles generated a political dynamism, particularly in West Germany, which profoundly affected both West-West and East-West relations. For the first time in recent years, he noted, a break had developed in transatlantic ties as a large section of Western public opinion demonstrated that it would no longer toe the line of Alliance policies without misgivings and without serious questioning. In his opinion, the future of Western security was challenged less by threats from the East than by the erosion of political cohesion in the West.[2]

In the United States, former Secretary of State Henry Kissinger warned in a widely circulated weekly news magazine that the depth of the divisions within NATO on East-West relations, defence strategy, arms control, and relations with the underdeveloped world is both unprecedented and unsettling. In his gloomy analysis, the absence of any intellectual or philosophical agreement was creating 'an exceedingly dangerous situation.'[3]

In September 1983, in his Alastair Buchan Memorial Lecture to the International Institute of Strategic Studies, NATO's new secretary general, Lord Carrington, described the Alliance as resting on a tripod: first, it needed strong democracies, and economies to match; second, it needed a sound and sufficient military deterrent; lastly, it needed a vision of the future and a practical policy to pursue that vision in the form of a strategy for dealing with the Soviet Union. In Carrington's opinion, the first two legs of the tripod were reasonably firm. The third was shakier, because NATO lacks a positive political strategy for dealing with the Russians and, in its absence, the Alliance could be thrown off balance by some essentially peripheral problem.[4] Certainly, there is abundant evidence to support Carrington's view.

Beginning with the Western reaction to the Soviet invasion and occupation of Afghanistan, through the Polish crisis (including the pipeline dispute), it has been apparent that the United States approach to East-West relations has often been markedly different from that of most of its allies. Divergences certainly existed during the administration of President Carter, but they became more numerous and more pronounced with the advent of an administration that was committed to a large defence build-up and was known to be suspicious of the Soviet Union, to regard the SALT II agreement as seriously flawed, and to be critical of détente, arguing that during the period of détente the advantages were all on the side of the Soviet Union, which continued its defence build-up.

One of the most striking divergences of views since the present United States administration took office in 1980 has been the widely divisive pipeline issue, on which its attitude appeared to be that, with the possible exception of arms control and grain sales, there was little to be gained from dealing with Moscow. Its view seemed to be that the allies should aim at hastening the collapse of the Soviet economy, should refrain from trade deals likely to improve the Soviet Union's security position, and should pursue a course which would eventually loosen Soviet control over Eastern Europe.

The European reaction to the administration's approach, as described by Pieter Dankert in an article in *Foreign Policy*,[5] reflected a view that was also widely held in Canada. Dankert observed that Western Europe refused to accept the United States thesis that the West was in a state of permanent conflict with the Soviet Union. Most European allies regarded as unacceptable and dangerous the idea that Alliance policies should be co-ordinated within a common strategy that was aimed at checking, countering, or undermining the Soviet system. While punitive measures such as those taken towards Soviet moves in Poland and Afghanistan can demonstrate condemnation, they cannot solve the longer-term problem of dealing with the Soviet Union. The West's policy towards Moscow requires both measures to ensure adequate defence and a willingness to continue communication in all areas. The desire for dialogue stems not from intimidation but from the knowledge that understanding and mutual confidence, rather than fear and uncertainty, provide the only basis for lasting stability.

Fortunately, the sharpness of the pipeline dispute was blunted by the skilful work of the American secretary of state and Canada's minister for external affairs at the special meeting of NATO foreign ministers convened near Montreal in the autumn of 1982. Following a very frank exchange, an informal agreement was reached that the whole range of East-West economic issues should be studied with a view to reaching an overall consensus. This accord in turn permitted the United States to back down by quietly removing the embargo it had earlier imposed unilaterally.

Once again the Alliance as an institution had shown its remarkable resilience and adaptability in facilitating the successful resolution of a potentially explosive issue. Moreover, in retrospect, the outcome represented something of a turning point in Alliance relationships. Not only was the new United States administration persuaded to back down in its efforts to impose its world view on its allies, but the agreement reached underlined the central importance of developing an agreed approach to relations with the Soviet Union, if only in the economic sphere. Moreover, it marked the beginning of a series of studies which culminated in the report on

East-West relations submitted to the anniversary meeting of foreign ministers in Washington.

Underlying differences of approach towards dealing with the Soviet Union were also apparent in respect of arms control and disarmament. Most of the allies, including Canada, were inclined to attach as much importance to efforts to negotiate balanced and verifiable arms control and disarmament agreements as they did to maintaining adequate defensive strength. By contrast, the overall impression left by the Reagan administration's statements and actions has been one of misgivings about the arms control process, coupled with an underlying belief that only a strengthened West could induce the Soviet Union to accommodate Western security interests.

Given these internal differences, it was a tribute to the Alliance's strength as an institution that it was able to implement the December 1979 two-track decision without seriously impairing its unity. This achievement was even more impressive if we accept Christoph Bertram's thesis that the decision was based on profound misunderstandings. He argued that nuclear weapons can only be a cure to a crisis of confidence in the Alliance, resulting from the emergence of strategic nuclear parity between the two superpowers, if there is trust in the security partnership. If that trust is lacking (for example, because of lack of confidence in American leadership), the nuclear weapons will be seen as disturbing rather than as reassuring. In his view, the second mistake was to believe that putting the missiles in an arms control context would make them more palatable to an anxious public. The result was that in the eyes of the public, progress was measured more by the willingness of the superpowers to compromise during the negotiations than by the condition and dynamics of the military balance. Clearly, the Soviet Union took advantage of this situation by developing negotiating positions which gave a false public impression of greater flexibility than the United States, but which in fact were designed to exclude the possibility of any Western deployment.

While the United States may not have played its cards particularly well during the negotiations, and while it may have left the impression with the European public that it was more interested in deployment than in an arms control agreement, the Soviet Union appears to have made an even more serious mistake in counting on public opposition, particularly in the Federal Republic of Germany, to prevent any deployment in the absence of agreement at the negotiating table. As a result, it had little option other than to withdraw from the talks when Western deployment materialized. Also, by setting unreasonable conditions for resumption, the Soviets undermined their claim that the United States was responsible for the lack of progress in arms control.

With respect to arms control in outer space, the position of the United States appeared to be less credible and represented a potential source of disunity in the Alliance. The Americans' unwillingness to engage in anti-satellite talks with the USSR and their announced intention to proceed with a vast research program designed to determine the feasibility of a space-based defensive system (SDI) has not been well received by most NATO members. Given the important implications these issues could have for the future of arms control, as well as for the viability of the British and French nuclear deterrents, the United States would be well advised to reconsider its approach.

Against the background of the missile debate, one is inclined to question Lord Carrington's confidence in the relative firmness of the second leg of his tripod – a sound and sufficient military deterrent. Henry Kissinger appears to believe that support for the deployment of the missiles would be increased if European leaders explained more clearly that the missiles were there to provide assurance of the United States' commitment. But as Bertram rightly points out, no amount of explaining and no review will be able to remove entirely the basic contradiction of extended deterrence – the theory that, for the sake of deterring an attack on Europe, the United States should be prepared to risk its own survival. Undoubtedly, what is required is an element of mutual trust, and this appears to be lacking.

Many observers maintain that confidence in current defence strategy would be increased if the Alliance reduced its reliance on nuclear weapons by increasing its conventional strength considerably. This is Kissinger's preferred solution, with the additional strength to be provided by the Europeans, who would assume principal responsibility for this aspect of Alliance defence. He maintains that such a strategy would not only have greater credibility in an age of superpower nuclear parity but, more importantly, that it would encourage other members to adopt a broader Alliance approach to international issues and to be less responsive to domestic pressure groups, which are often unduly critical of the United States.

Given the economic realities of the 1980s, is such an approach practical? There is evidence of a tendency in Europe, and in Canada as well, to attribute many of the West's economic difficulties to high American interest rates, which are believed to be caused by excessive spending on defence which has driven up the United States' already huge deficit. In any event, unless economic conditions in the other allied countries improve, it will be exceedingly difficult for national governments to increase their share of defence spending in order to reduce reliance on nuclear weapons. Meanwhile, the impression is widespread in the United States, particularly in the Congress, that the allies are not contributing their fair share to NATO while refusing to support American foreign policies. American frustration is further exacerbated by economic disputes with the European Communities; these disputes tend to reinforce the feeling of many Americans about the unbalanced nature of a relationship in which Europeans feel free to impose trade restrictions while going along as military dependents. In short, any assessment of the strength and cohesion of the Alliance as an institution must take account of the interaction between economic and defence policies. Article II of the treaty, it will be recalled, was concerned with the economic dimension of the Alliance: 'They [the parties] will seek to eliminate conflict in their international economic policies and will encourage economic collaboration between any or all of them.'

The continuing crisis in the Persian Gulf highlights the importance of these issues for the Alliance. The Reagan administration, unlike its predecessor, appears to have adopted a more realistic conception of Soviet objectives in the area. It also appears to accept what has tended to be the assessment of most of its allies, including Canada, that stability in the Gulf is affected more by local regional developments than by the menace of Soviet military power, and that the direct involvement of American military forces would only make matters worse.

By contrast, few allies would share the American view regarding the magnitude of the Soviet threat in other areas, especially in Central

America. While there is general agreement that NATO must be concerned with the danger to its security on a global basis, the authors of *Canada and Western Security* quite rightly point out that any attempt to involve Alliance members in a collective effort outside the treaty area would put too much strain on its cohesion. Nor would the idea of setting up small groups of countries be a desirable approach, since it would serve to reinforce an existing tendency to divide members into an inner and an outer group. As the authors note, the United States is pretty much alone in being able to cope militarily with this kind of problem.[6] In fact, a procedure has already been established in NATO that if national forces are removed from the treaty area, arrangements will be made, following consultations, to ensure that sufficient military capabilities remain in the area.

Stimulated by the pipeline dispute, the Alliance embarked on a series of studies with the main purpose of designing a broad strategy for dealing with the Soviet Union. The lack of such a strategy, which has been noted by Lord Carrington and others, has been central to a number of internal disputes in NATO which, over recent years, have tended to erode the mutual respect and confidence that are so essential to NATO's strength and cohesion. Formal authorization to proceed was given by the foreign ministers in Brussels in December 1983, when they instructed the Permanent Council to prepare, for the anniversary meeting in Washington, a thorough appraisal of East-West relations with a view 'to achieving a more constructive East-West dialogue.'[7]

Canadian concern regarding the need for a more constructive dialogue with the Soviet Union was underlined publicly and privately on several occasions by Prime Minister Trudeau, especially in his discussions with world leaders during his peace initiative. Moreover, the secretary of state for external affairs and other Canadian officials played a prominent part in the deliberations at the December 1983 ministerial meeting and at the subsequent sessions of the Permanent Council when the report was being prepared.

Judging from the statement issued by the foreign ministers in Washington at the anniversary meeting on 31 May, considerable progress was made in developing a strategy which essentially reaffirms the balanced approach contained in the Harmel Report of 1967, i.e., the maintenance of adequate military strength and political solidarity and, on that basis, the pursuit of a more stable East-West relationship through dialogue and co-operation. Despite fundamental differences between East and West, the report recognizes the existence of areas of common interest, which should be built upon in the promotion of a more constructive dialogue 'with a view to achieving genuine détente.'[8]

A number of points consistently stressed by Canada are included in the statement, which is strikingly devoid of the harsh references to the Soviet Union that are often found in NATO communiqués. In short, if the document accurately reflects the substance of the main report (which presumably is confidential), it represents quite an achievement and grounds for encouragement regarding the future course of the policies of individual members. It remains to be seen, of course, whether endorsement of the statement by United States Secretary of State George Shultz represents a change in the American approach. Certainly, there was less anti-Soviet rhetoric emanating from Washington. President Reagan, in fact, appeared to be veering in the other direction. Speaking to the press following the NATO meeting in Washington, he was reported to have said that the United States and its NATO allies recognized that 'there is no more important consideration than the development of a better working relationship with the Soviet Union.'

In any event, it would seem to be in Canada's interest and in the interests of like-minded allies (e.g., the Federal Republic of Germany) to make every effort to ensure that the principles and recommendations in the report are translated in practice into policies by all members, and particularly by the United States.

One means of encouraging members to comply with the report's recommendations would be to intensify the practice of consultation in NATO. In his analysis of the strains in the Alliance, Kissinger concluded that improved consultation would not help. He argued that real consultation works only when the side being consulted has a capacity for independent action. In such circumstances, each side takes the other seriously. Otherwise, consultation becomes a briefing in which agreement amounts to acquiescence, for want of an alternative.[9] However logical, Kissinger's argument overlooks two key considerations. First, apart from the United States, few NATO members have a capacity for independent action in the security area of arms control and defence. Second, it is self-evident that effective co-operation in NATO depends largely on the extent to which member governments, in their own policies and actions, take into consideration the interests of the Alliance.

This matter of co-operation in the Alliance was the subject of a report of a special committee of three foreign ministers (Lester Pearson, Halvard Lange of Norway, and Gaetano Martino of Italy) following the Suez Crisis of 1956. One of its major conclusions was that effective co-operation requires the acceptance of the obligation of consultation and the development of appropriate practices as a normal part of government activity. In their view, 'consultation means more than letting the Council know about national decisions that have already been taken; or trying to enlist support for those decisions. It means the discussion of problems collectively ... before national positions become fixed. At best this will result in collective decisions on matters of common interest ...; at least it will ensure that no action is taken by one member without a knowledge of the views of the others.'[10]

Perhaps it is unrealistic to set one's sights too high in relation to improvements in consultation. Obviously, much will depend on the political will of member governments, and there may be bureaucratic impediments to advance consultation, such as the complexities of the American governmental process and rivalries within the executive branch. There may also be cases in which allies would prefer not to be consulted (e.g., in relation to the Persian Gulf), since the very act of consultation entails an implicit obligation to get involved in one way or another. Nevertheless, to the extent that many of the current strains in the Alliance have had their origin in divergences over East-West relations, and to the extent that these may have been largely resolved in the 1984 report, an intensification of the practice of consultation along the lines suggested by the 'committee of three' could serve to encourage adherence to policies that are consistent with the agreed strategy.

Arms control is an area of increasing importance to the Alliance. It is a particularly tricky area, given the growing public interest in the subject and the implications of negotiating proposals for the defensive strength of the member countries, particularly when nuclear weapons are involved. As a result, the role which consultation plays is often critical to the maintenance of broad allied support for American negotiating proposals and for confidence in American leadership. During the negotiations on the Intermediate Nuclear Force (INF), new procedures were devised and regularly used for intra-Alliance consultation. Unfortunately, for reasons that are still not entirely clear, the United States administration did not fulfil its obligation to consult its allies on the one development which could have led to a breakthrough (the proposal discussed by the American negotiator, Paul Nitze, with his Soviet counterpart during their now famous 'walk in the woods'). On the other hand, the record of consultation in respect of the Vienna talks on Mutual and Balanced Force Reductions (MBFR) and the Conference on Security and Co-operation in Europe (CSCE) has so far been generally satisfactory. The need for a considerable improvement in consultation is evident with respect to the use of space for defence purposes. Here the danger of wide divergence between the United States and the Alliance is very real. As a minimum, the United States should attempt to explain more convincingly to its partners why it does not wish to participate in anti-satellite talks with the USSR and the rationale for proceeding with President Reagan's SDI, or 'star wars' proposal, the future consequences of which could undermine allied deterrence policy and cast in doubt the whole future of strategic arms control.

Given the current lack of confidence in American leadership and allied misgivings regarding the exceptionally heavy emphasis it places on increased military power, the United States' failure to consult adequately with its allies on this kind of issue and/or a determination to proceed regardless of allied opposition could have very serious consequences for the future cohesion and viability of the Alliance.

NOTES

1 R. B. Byers et al., *Canada and Western Security* (Toronto 1982).
2 Christoph Bertram, 'Europe and America in 1983,' in *America and the World*, special issue of *Foreign Affairs* 62, no 2, 1984.
3 Henry Kissinger, 'A Plan to Reshape NATO,' *Time*, 5 March 1984, 26-30.
4 Lord Carrington, 'The Alastair Buchan Memorial Lecture,' *Survival* 25, no 4 (July/August 1983), 146-64.

5 Pieter Dankert, 'Europe Together, America Apart,' *Foreign Policy* 53 (Winter 1983-84), 18-33.
6 Byers et al., *Canada and Western Security*, 14.
7 Communiqué of 9 December 1983, *Texts of Communiqués and Declarations Issued After Meetings Held at Ministerial Level During 1983* (Brussels nd), 33-38.
8 'The Future Tasks of the Alliance,' appendix to the communiqué of the ministerial meeting, Brussels, 13-14 December 1967. *NATO Final Communiqués 1949-1974* (Brussels nd), 198-202. Communiqué of 31 May 1984 in *Texts of Communiqués and Declarations Issued After Meetings Held at Ministerial Level During 1984* (Brussels nd), 17-23.
9 Kissinger, 'A Plan to Reshape NATO.'
10 Appendix to final communiqué, 14 December 1956, *NATO Final Communiqués 1949-1974*.

Canada and the Reform of NATO

GERALD WRIGHT

It is not unusual to discover forces within an international institution that are working towards its transformation. These forces frequently appear to gather strength as an institution ages and as it becomes harder to make its underlying political purpose sound convincing in contemporary terms. Shifts in power and influence between states, the motivations of the primary political actors, and underlying social trends all appear to be out of consonance with arrangements for allocating decision-making authority and associated responsibilities. What cannot be perceived as clearly is whether these arrangements have become so much part of the warp and woof of the prevailing order (indeed, whether the dangers they were intended to meet are not dead but merely sleeping) that it would be better to live with an antiquated and anomalous structure in preference to the upheaval that drastic reform could bring.

Structural anomalies within NATO have been growing more pronounced as the postwar era has worn on. The most notable of these is the extent to which Western Europe continues to rely on the United States for its security, despite the considerable economic advance it has made since the devastation of the 1940s. Admittedly, the population of the European NATO members (325 million in 1979) is a bit behind that of the WTO (372 million). The Soviet Union must, however, make allowance for the unreliability of its allies and must also take into consideration two more potential adversaries, the United States (230 million) and China (one billion). In any case, the gross domestic product of NATO Europe is substantially greater than that of the WTO countries. By any measure of national power, Western Europe should not be having to rely on its transatlantic partner for a major portion of its conventional defence, land, sea and air, as well as for leadership in analysing its own security needs and in negotiating arms control agreements.

The Alliance's structural deficiencies appear more serious in the light of its present discontents. Political tensions at the surface of NATO often appear enough to make its bolts and rivets fly apart. A large number of salient issues, ranging from relations with the Soviet bloc and arms control to unrest in the Third World, are viewed quite differently by the governments of Europe and that of the United States. The peace movement has forced a number of European governments to break ranks with the Alliance and has made an even more powerful impact on several of Europe's largest opposition parties. On the economic front, the interest rate policies of the Federal Reserve Board have worsened wounds already opened up by transatlantic trade wars and by charges and countercharges of protectionism.

The picture of Alliance disunity has evoked well-thought-out proposals for the reform of NATO from a number of distinguished analysts, among them Henry Kissinger and the late Hedley Bull. The latter wrote from a European perspective.[1] He sought to break loose from the tensions, inconsistencies, and imbalances of the postwar period by transferring to Europe a greater measure of responsibility for its own defence and a concomitantly greater measure of the cost. Bull found powerfully attractive the idea of a regional society taking its destiny into its own hands, thinking through its own strategic priorities, and bearing the costs of its own decisions. To be dependent upon another power for security is both demeaning and stultifying. Moreover, he contended that if the European public were able to distinguish clearly between United States policies, on the one hand, and the policies governing its own security, on the other, this would not only be a healthy development in itself but would lead to greater public support for defence.

Bull would retain the shelter of the NATO umbrella, together with a nuclear guarantee of Europe by the United States and the presence of United States forces on the continent. The novel part of his prescription is a call for stronger European conventional forces and an enhanced nuclear role for Europe, including firm 'two key' arrangements for all American nuclear weapons remaining in Europe, steps towards building a European nuclear force on the basis of Franco-British co-operation, and the establishment of a European Nuclear Planning Committee, analogous to NATO's Nuclear Planning Group (NPG). Bull would even draw West Germany into nuclear policy-making and would propel the European allies into developing their own 'out-of-area' capability to defend their extraregional interests. In his view, these innovations are the essential preconditions of a Europeanist policy, which would diverge from an American policy in that it would place heavy emphasis on preserving the benefits of détente. In passing, Bull noted that such a bifurcation of the Alliance would pose serious problems for Canada.[2]

Henry Kissinger followed the same line as Hedley Bull, up to a point.[3] Europe should have much greater responsibility for its own security, grounding its judgements on its own analyses of the strategic situation and, in particular, taking over the major responsibility for conventional ground defence. SACEUR should be a European, and Europeans should play the leading role in arms control talks dealing with weapons on their own soil. The present complement of United States ground forces should remain, but only if the Europeans seize the opportunity to mount an effective conventional defence, thereby alleviating their own nuclear anxieties. At the same time, Dr Kissinger appeared to believe that greater reliance on conventional forces would eradicate the Alliance's old bugbear, the issue of nuclear control.

The fundamental point of difference between Bull and Kissinger is that whereas the former saw structural reform as the precondition of healthy policy divergence, the latter believed that increasing Europe's responsibility and unity within NATO would promote closer co-operation with the United States. In particular, there would be less temptation to display independence of the superpower ally. Kissinger even held out a hope that basing NATO deployments on a more sensible and up-to-date rationale would help moderate European pacifism and American isolationism, or at least would not exacerbate them. In the Kissingerian hall of horrors, there is no spectre so dreadful as that of public opinion intruding on foreign policy. In this case, neutralizing public opinion was viewed as doubly imperative because of the Soviet Union's proven capability to exploit Western disunity and weakness of will.

The idea of Western Europeans taking more of their defence problem into their own hands has received a good deal of serious consideration in official circles. Most notably, President François Mitterrand has become an ardent advocate of closer French-German co-operation on military matters, and he has coupled this advocacy with some specific proposals, such as that of a European military reconnaissance space satellite. A number of interpretations of the French president's démarche are possible. One is that he is simply trying to bolster France's influence in the management and conduct of Europe's defence. A second is that he is convinced that Western Europe must be seen to be pulling its weight if the United States is to remain committed to its security. The third is that he is alarmed by the prospect of West Germany, already infected by neutralism, slipping away from the Western Alliance. Developing closer consultations and a few common projects with his partner across the Rhine would afford the opportunity of checking this tendency at the same time as reviving a co-operative spirit and a dynamism that have recently been sadly lacking within the European Communities.

The government of West German Chancellor Helmut Kohl has its own reasons to push for greater European self-reliance within NATO. The French president's conception of the Alliance as resting on two pillars is, however, discomfiting to the West Germans. The Kohl government has made clear that the primary importance it places upon the defence relationship with the United States sets definite limits to how far it is prepared to go in joint endeavours with France. Hans-Dietrich Genscher, the Federal Republic's foreign minister, has also been at pains to stress that a new defence relationship within Europe is not intended as a device whereby West Germany will be ushered into a nuclear role.

There are two related subjects that are currently high on the agendas of West European governments. First is the long-standing issue of rationalizing arms production. The NATO Eurogroup, which is made up of the European defence ministers with the exception of the French, recently decided to hand this issue to the Independent European Programme Group, which includes France. The second agenda item is the effort to revitalize the Western European Union (WEU), which was set up in 1954 by Great Britain, France, Belgium, The Netherlands, Luxembourg, Italy, and West Germany for the purpose of facilitating West Germany's entry into NATO.

Can we expect the integrationist stirrings in Europe to leave more than a ripple in the sand? On the one hand, the measures currently being discussed by European governments are exceedingly modest. They can, of course, be justified as strengthening NATO, and indeed they are perceived this way by many European leaders.

Furthermore, recent history hangs a question mark over Western Europe's progress in the direction of defence integration. The French proposal of a European Defence Community came to naught in 1954. Britain and France have never been able to co-ordinate nuclear weapons development, despite the economic inducement to do so. Helmut Schmidt and Valéry Giscard d'Estaing are reported to have been attracted to the idea of defence integration, but their discussions never had any visible result. The roadblocks are many, psychological and political. There is a strongly held point of view that a Western Europe more independent in defence matters and, in particular, with an expanded nuclear role, would witness a re-emergence of the old rivalries that so often have rent the continent.[4] Many Europeans are deeply convinced that they cannot, in fact, do without the United States.

On the other hand, given the Alliance's somewhat shaky condition, these tentative moves bear watching. Conceptions of Europe as a neutral buffer between the superpowers, or as an independent 'third force,' have not lost their grip on the imaginations of fringe politicians and polemicists. Who can tell what currents could be set in motion by even a few steps in the direction of a more unified defence structure? While President Mitterrand and Chancellor Kohl may be staunch Atlanticists, their countrymen on left and right wings may be lying in wait to take over Europeanization and divert it to their own parochial ends.

Between these two extremes, there is a range of possible outcomes that Canadian policy makers should address:

- a modest measure of European defence integration, along the lines discussed by the governments of France and the Federal Republic;
- a more cohesive Atlantic Alliance based on structural reform, as proposed by Henry Kissinger;
- a bifurcated Alliance, as advocated by Hedley Bull.

The manner in which Canada would have to adjust to any one of these outcomes can be better understood in light of the rationale behind this country's energetic pursuit of the North Atlantic Treaty in 1948-49. The active involvement of the United States in a workable system of collective security was considered to be absolutely essential to the restoration of the political and economic health of the democracies of Western Europe. Furthermore, as Lester Pearson wrote in *Foreign Affairs* in 1951, 'If Washington "went it alone," where would Ottawa go?'[5] At the same time, a multilateral alliance was clearly preferred over a unilateral guarantee of Western Europe by the United States, since it was believed that Canada would be advantaged by dealing with its powerful southern neighbour in a multilateral framework rather than bilaterally. Multilateralism was entrenched all the more firmly as a cardinal principle of postwar foreign policy because it neatly synthesized Canada's co-operative orientation and its ingrained suspicion of entangling bilateral involvements, both of which occasionally conflicting urges were born of the country's imperial experience.

Would defence integration in Europe represent the final defeat of Canada's multilateral principle, as far as Western security was concerned? How would the Canadian public's support of the Alliance be affected by evidence of the Europeans taking greater responsibility for their own defence? How would Canada's effectiveness within the Alliance be altered by structural reform? What would Europe's newfound resolve and cohesion do to the conduct of Canada's relations with the United States? In short, if Europe were to 'go it alone,' where would Canada go?

Incremental integration in Europe would amount to continuing official conversations, some joint projects, a co-ordinated effort to make weapons production a genuine two-way street, and, just possibly, a joint resolve to tackle the imbalance in conventional forces in Europe. Indeed, it is difficult to contemplate the Europeans mounting stronger conventional land forces in the absence of some kind of concert between Paris and Bonn. France and the Federal Republic are, after all, the two major NATO powers that cling to compulsory military service. Longtime German opposition to any suggestion of prolonged conventional war in central Europe would have to be overcome, but the recent nuclear travail may have made this easier to accomplish. It could certainly be argued convincingly that Europe would be a good deal safer if NATO were able to return to the concept of flexible response that was originally enunciated by Robert McNamara in Athens in 1962, whereby the onus was to be placed on the adversary to make the decision to escalate to the nuclear level.[6]

Canadian public opinion is likely to be favourably impressed by the picture of Europeans getting their own house in order and is likely to evidence more support for substantial improvements in Canada's contribution to the defence of Western Europe. However, the movement of public opinion would probably not be enough to bulk large in the government's consideration of defence policy. It would, in fact, be more than compensated for by a reduction in American pressure to strengthen the forces in Europe. In other respects, the impact on bilateral relations would be of small significance. The most noteworthy result could be an enhancement of Canada's potential effectiveness within the Alliance, because of the greater value that the Europeans would place on this country's commitment to their defence. Their primary preoccupation would be not to let their assumption of a greater burden diminish by one whit the United States' commitment to their security. In consequence, Canada's commitment, however modest, would mean all the more to them, and Canada's potential leverage, should the government choose to make use of it, could be markedly increased.

Those who have lived through the Alliance's internal traumas over the past decade will be understandably sceptical of Henry Kissinger's scenario for a more cohesive Alliance. Nonetheless, it is an attractive scenario, insofar as it holds out the promise of a successfully co-ordinated strategy for the management of East-West relations. As far as Canada is concerned, of course, a lot would depend on the policies around which the Alliance would coalesce. If, for example, the United States were to insist upon taking a Reaganite line, a maverick Canadian government might find itself at odds with public opinion, which has been fairly consistent in its support of NATO over the years. Whatever the political complexion of the United States administration, Canada would be unlikely to feel comfortable in an alliance in which the main lines of policy were negotiated between the European bloc and the United States and in which not much attention was paid to the views of the odd man out. Nor, presumably, would there be room to manoeuvre, to build temporary coalitions of like-minded NATO members so as to temper the policies and actions of the superpower. Canada's effectiveness within the Alliance would be minimal, and far from NATO serving to aid Canada in its bilateral dealings with the United States, the near-monolithic unity of the major members of the Alliance would add moral and political weight to the demands that Washington placed on Ottawa. In many respects, a more cohesive alliance resting on the twin pillars of Europe and the United States would be the worst possible outcome for Canada. The Alliance would feel like a straitjacket and, at the same time, it would be exceedingly difficult to summon up the political energy to release the cords.

Hedley Bull's prescription for a bifurcated Alliance may not sound very different from current intra-Alliance divisions, which are largely due to differing European and American conceptions of détente. The situation would not be the same, however, for Western Europe's policies towards the Eastern bloc would proceed from a strengthened institutional base and would be informed by a consciousness of in-dependence and self-reliance.

In such circumstances, it is quite likely that Canadian public opinion would turn from general support of the Alliance to a fairly agnostic position, and there would be a more attentive audience for the argument that greater attention should be paid to home defence, including the protection of Arctic sovereignty and the surveillance of coastlines. The perception of Western Europe handling its own defence, and doing so in the service of its own distinctive political purposes, would certainly make much less tenable the proposition that Canada's security should be defended on the European continent, and there would be increasingly vocal demands to bring the boys back home.

Canada's effectiveness within the newly bifurcated NATO would depend on whether there was room for a go-between, doubtless shar-ing some of the perceptions of both sides, to keep communication between them open. An alternative, and more compelling, possibility is that Canada would be caught in the middle between the conflicting demands of the two major constituents of the Alliance. Such a role, with its attendant frustrations, might not be sustainable for very long, and it might be expected that the country's affiliation with NATO would gradually be de-emphasized until it became a mere matter of ritual. Moreover, on the bilateral front the effects would be wholly bad, for the United States, shorn of its European allies, could be expected to try to draw its continental partners closer and to seek solace in their solidarity.

Although Canadians might well approve a measure of 'Europeanization,' they have good reason to attack one of its strongest psychological supports: the beguiling image of the dumbbell, the idea that NATO is essentially a compact between 'a mythical being called "Europe" and a fabulous creature called "America." '[7] Judging by the possible effect on Canada of more advanced states of European defence integration, there is a strong case for recalling the Alliance to its original principle of multilateralism. The proposition that there is value in diversity, that a complex web of alignments between allies is preferable to the dumbbell, is one that could be put forward on both altruistic and selfish grounds.

Even if the concept of a multilateral alliance were to be more carefully developed and articulated, it is doubtful that Canada could, by its own efforts, move its allies very far in that direction. The image of the dumbbell is difficult to dislodge. Nevertheless, as pointed out earlier in this chapter, there are powerful forces within Europe that will exert a drag on the movement towards an independent defence structure. If Canadian political leaders were once again to become persistent and persuasive advocates of multilateralism, they could usefully bolster these forces and help nudge the Alliance back to its original path.

NOTES

1 Hedley Bull, 'European Self-Reliance and the Reform of NATO,' *Foreign Affairs* 61, no 4 (Spring 1983), 874-92.
2 'A division of the Alliance between American and European pillars,

moreover, would be unwelcome in Canada, whose interest in maintaining a European defence commitment would be more difficult to sustain.' *Ibid.*, 890.

3 Henry Kissinger, 'A Plan to Reshape NATO,' *Time*, 5 March 1984, 26-30.

4 Josef Joffe, 'Europe's American Pacifier,' *Foreign Policy* 54 (Spring 1984), 64-82.

5 Lester Pearson, 'The Development of Canadian Foreign Policy,' *Foreign Affairs* 30, no 1 (October 1951), 26.

6 David N. Schwartz, NATO's *Nuclear Dilemmas* (Washington 1983), 156-65.

7 John W. Holmes, 'The Dumbbell Won't Do,' *Foreign Policy* 50 (Spring 1983), 3.

Canada, NATO, and Western Security

JOHN W. HOLMES

Is our faith in NATO justified? Is it fulfilling those hopes we have had for the multilateral way? Some doubts have been cast on the effectiveness of the consultative role of the Alliance. Clear evidence of this is necessary if the public is to be convinced. The problem is, of course, that the effectiveness of NATO in compromise and co-ordination depends to a large extent on the confidentiality of the procedure. If Canadian diplomacy is consistently loud, it is apt to be ineffective. Perhaps what is most required is a recognition on the part of officials and of the public that both sides of this paradox have to be taken into consideration.

The idea that NATO is stuck in the grooves of postwar assumptions persists. But on the whole NATO has adapted reasonably well to circumstances, and in so doing it has assisted in the alteration of the perceptions and policies of governments. In support of this view, one need only cite the truly remarkable transformation of Alliance thinking from confrontation and the simple aim of superior power to the acceptance of détente, mutual deterrence, and negotiation with the arch-antagonist, the Warsaw Treaty Organization (WTO). Rather than thinking of NATO as a means for preserving the *status quo*, it would be wise to recognize the way in which it has managed change. The principal value of the Alliance lies in the manner in which it

cf.
Sokolsky + Jockel : principle value is
collective defence.

provides an agency for consultation and a continual review of circumstances and policies, and there has been enough accomplished in recent years to encourage some confidence.

Should the aim of NATO be a total concert of policies? To what extent is a common front on all issues desirable? Is there not advantage in diversity of approach on some world issues, especially on those outside the NATO area? The imposition of common policies would certainly create intense difficulties for member governments on the domestic front. While the Alliance's aim may not be alignment on all issues, and while there is an argument for diversity, what is needed is agreement on grand strategy vis-à-vis the Soviet Union. This has been the main cause of difference between the United States and its allies. (It might be added that it is never difficult to get the Americans to agree to diversity in principle, but they usually object on high moral grounds when it actually happens.)

The relative success of NATO consultation emerges clearly if one lists the substantive problems which the Alliance is now facing:[1]
- the whole range of East-West issues, including particularly the question of Western objectives vis-à-vis the USSR and the balance between defence and dialogue;
- defence strategy, including the impact of nuclear parity on the doctrine of flexible response and the balance between nuclear and conventional weaponry, where the role of technology is important;
- arms control: how to keep negotiations going and to keep up with technological progress; and
- the relationship between economic and defence policies.

Consideration of how to deal with these problems raises a number of procedural and organizational questions:
- the process of consultation;
- the relation of a superpower with its allies;
- European defence co-operation; and
- possible structural reform in NATO.

While there has been erosion in the Alliance relationship, it would take a great deal of erosion to bring about Hedley Bull's scenario[2] of an autonomous Europe – something, for example, like a Soviet attack on Norway without an American response. The lowest common denominator for Alliance consensus has traditionally been fear of the Soviet Union, but now this is the principal area of contention, so the increasing intensity of the East-West conflict is paralleled by increasing intensity of dissent in NATO. This has inevitably encouraged a greater tendency to consolidation in Europe. The consequences would logically be an increase in the conventional build-up, but here the problem of higher costs supervenes. If there is to be an increase of conventional forces in Europe, then an increased contribution by Canada would be doubly welcomed. One way of trying to cope with these pressures is to push ahead with the Mutual and Balanced Force Reductions (MBFR) negotiations in Vienna; but relief is not likely to come soon from this quarter. The Europeans want to decouple intra-European détente from the troubled relationship between the United States and the USSR, and they are trying to do this within the framework of the Conference on Security and Co-operation in Europe (CSCE). They might even want to carry this aim into the MBFR talks, though the chances of such decoupling would be far less in the MBFR framework because the United States is far more involved in them than in the CSCE forum.

There is 'no other way' that other members of the Alliance can have influence in Washington except through persuasion. This effort will not always be successful, of course. The tendency of the United States – and not just the present administration – has been to follow its own lead. Domestic pressures, the nature of the governmental system, and the insistence of the American media on immediate responses from the administration mean that the president acts as he deems appropriate, without pausing to talk with his allies. For example, at the NATO ministerial meeting in Washington in May 1984, it was agreed that a pledge of the non-use of force could be held as a bargaining chip with the USSR. Yet a few days later President Reagan saw fit, for various political reasons, to make the public pledge before an audience in Dublin.[3] Nevertheless, there has been progress in getting the United States into some agreement on the economic strategies to be adopted towards the Soviet bloc. In Brussels there has been intense study of the efficacy of sanctions, as well as discussion of whether the concept of 'economic warfare' is applicable, and about the value of cultural and scientific exchanges.

It has sometimes been charged that Canadians have been led into policies which the public has not adequately considered, let alone approved, and that through NATO Canada has surrendered control over its defence policy to a body managed by the great powers, without giving Canadians the opportunity to debate the decision. Clearly, the government has not given very helpful leadership in explaining some of the issues involved. The hasty decision in 1957 to go along with NORAD, without even parliamentary discussion, is a case in point. Another example is the more recent acquiescence, in the NATO Council, in the decision to place Cruise and Pershing missiles in Europe.[4] In both cases, the consequences of the commitment were debated only after the commitment had been made.

On the other hand, this loss of control may be regarded as the price that a weaker power has to pay for collective defence, the option that Canada deliberately chose in the 1940s as the most practical and also the cheapest way of defending an enormous country. Canada is not bound to accept all NATO decisions, but it does have to recognize that it can rarely veto them and that it can only resign once. In the interests of non-proliferation, Canada opted out of a nuclear role in the Alliance, just as Norway and Denmark did. However, Canadians should recognize that the strength of the Alliance on which they depend would be weakened if there was too much diversity and too much opting out. There is always the fear that the United States might be encouraged to do a little opting out itself.

In order to explain, though not necessarily to defend, the problems of governmental leadership, one can cite the controversial Canadian decision in December 1979 to endorse NATO strategy on Cruise missiles – a decision that was to haunt later governments. The decision was taken at a time when the government of Prime Minister Joe Clark was facing imminent collapse and when Secretary of State for External Affairs Flora MacDonald was coping secretly with the Canadian ramifications of the Teheran hostages. With the fall of the Clark government, the new Liberal administration had to implement the commitment. In these circumstances, Canada did not make an adequate contribution to the two-track decision, and public debate was lacking (but these are the realities of government in all countries that cherish democracy). Several cabinet sessions were devoted to the decision, however, and its implications were carefully studied by the bureaucrats.

Questions of arms control and strategy are extraordinarily complex, and, with the best of intentions, it is not always easy to set out the alternative choices to the politicians or the general public. One may envy the wide-open debates in Washington, but the Americans can afford to take their time because they are a decisive (often *the* decisive) power. But it should be remembered that they cause their allies acute problems because of their 'division of powers'; their administration's inability, after negotiation with other governments, to commit the United States is a form of constitutional self-indulgence that would not be tolerated in any lesser power.

As for the charge that NATO, an association of supposedly equal powers, sometimes acts undemocratically, one can point to the resistance by the Dutch to the placement of missiles on their soil. NATO seeks to get a common approach when consensus is possible – there is no voting on non-procedural issues – but, obviously, there cannot be perfect equality of decision-making in a military alliance in which one member, the United States, has the overall decisive forces and in which another member, West Germany, occupies the critical ground in Europe. How to make the best of these inexorable facts of life is the underlying structural problem for which no formal provisions have ever been found.

In order to comprehend the dumbbell concept, one needs to assess the realities of European 'integration.' There is not likely to be a dramatic change in the shape of the Alliance, nor are the Europeans likely to go far in the direction of autonomy. Still, Canadians must be prepared for eventualities, because there has to be a balance between European self-reliance and dependence on NATO. Reflecting on these strains serves to illustrate Canada's unique role in NATO, for there are contradictions it has to face. Greater European military independence would give Canada good reason to withdraw its expensive forces from Europe and to concentrate on defending the North American sector. On the other hand, because such a move would tend to isolate Canada in one wing of what is supposed to be a two-continent alliance, there might be an even stronger case for keeping one armed foot in Europe.

The dumbbell concept of NATO as a deal between 'America' and 'Europe' is probably more of a public perception than an accurate description of the way the multilateral alliance really works. The table in Brussels is round. There is no European military force and, on issues of policy, no single European or North American view. On the issues which supposedly divide the two continents, Canada is often closer to the Europeans, while Prime Minister Thatcher and President Reagan have many attitudes in common. The dumbbell assumption clearly poses problems for Canada, but, more important, it has aggravated transatlantic tensions.

For Canada, there have been diplomatic problems caused by the preliminary caucusing of the European Communities' members to establish a common front before talking with the other allies. This has been done at the United Nations and at sessions of the CSCE. A strong and united Western Europe might conceivably be a useful force in international security, but it is doubtful if there could be adequate consensus for anything but a timid and irresolute voice, one that would in fact be less confident than the voice of Germany or France or Britain on its own. For Canadians, whose traditional partners have been the smaller European states, it is a diplomatic handicap to be shut out of consultations at the formative stage. Inevitably, this encourages Canadians to look elsewhere for collaborators, and the North Atlantic factor in Canadian policy is correspondingly weakened.

What are the real prospects for European 'autonomy'? While this might be a promising avenue, it will not likely be achieved by the Europeans on their own. The United States would have to take a lead. If the Americans thought it in their interest to promote European responsibility in this way, there would have to be trade-offs. The Europeans would have to accept wider responsibilities for security outside the NATO area. It is not likely that the United States Congress would be sympathetic to making things easier for the Europeans unless there was a better understanding of the burdens sustained by the United States. On the other hand, the Americans would have to be more willing (by opening up technology, for example) to make it feasible for the Europeans to increase their conventional capabilities. They would also have to moderate their unilateral policy-making.

What is called 'European integration' might be better described as intergovernmentalism and introspection, rather than integration. Such cohesion as the Europeans have achieved might once have been attributable to fear of the USSR, but now it is inspired more by fear of the consequences of United States policy. As for sharing the burdens outside NATO, that would probably mean having to endorse United States policies, thus leading to further irritation within the

Alliance. The possibility of getting common action in such places as the Persian Gulf is exceedingly doubtful. In any case, Canada, which would have little hope of a say in the strategy, should not feel compelled to join in.

But which 'Europe' are we talking about, and do we mean autonomy or autarky? There are many cross-cut divisions in Europe besides East and West. The division between North and South is deep-rooted, and the cement which has held Europeans together has been the presence of the North American allies. On the other hand, the problem for the Europeans in general – and for Canada as well – is that the United States is becoming an increasingly expensive ally.[5] One thing driving the Europeans in quest of autonomy is the need to control their costs. There is also at present the diplomatic cost of being seen as allies of Washington. It is not only the Saudis who have had to avoid appearing as front-line allies of the Reagan administration in the Middle East. This has also been of particular concern to Europeans, and not only with respect to the present administration.

Three possible motives for increased European interest in defence integration may be suggested. In the first place, there is the concern over apparent trends towards neutralism in Germany and an anxiety to tie that country more securely to the European defence apparatus. Secondly, defence integration may be seen as a tactical way of getting France back into a closer military alignment with NATO. In addition, it would be a way of making defence programs more salable to European publics by 'putting a European mantle over NATO.' Finally, it might help in the removal of some of the constraints on German security policy that were imposed by the Western European Union (WEU) in 1955. Dissatisfaction with United States leadership is certainly an element, but it should be understood that European leaders see these moves in terms of an adjunct to NATO, rather than as a successor to it.

When the French speak of a European 'pillar,' no doubt they see it in terms of the dumbbell concept. The French have always pressed for the four main powers to have a special directoral role in the Alliance, and they have always been opposed in this by Canada, Italy, and the smaller powers. The dumbbell might be in Canada's interest if it led to a stronger NATO. Canada would like some redressing of the balance of leadership away from the United States. Greater European co-operation in defence production could give Canada a wider choice of weapons, some alternatives to American systems. However, such co-operation would create yet another subgroup in NATO, caucusing independently and leaving Canada on the outside looking in. Not only the Canadians but the Norwegians and the Turks, who are also outside the European Communities, would be alienated. This kind of transatlantic division could seriously weaken the Alliance by creating a larger group of the disaffected. Another matter of concern is that Britain's and France's autonomous development of their nuclear capacity is proceeding to a stage beyond deterrence and might thereby make the chance for arms control virtually impossible. The non-proliferation agreement would be lost if some understanding were not reached before the British and French completed their 'modernization.' This, it would seem, would be a challenge to the ability of the United States and the USSR to 'manage' a nuclear world order.

How best, one might ask, can Canada seek to fit into a structure which is or is perceived to be increasingly bilateral in shape? Would this best be done by seeking a 'special relationship' with the United States in what would formally or informally be regarded as the North American sector? This is an alternative that Canada has always viewed sceptically, but its options may be limited. European solidarity and American intolerance could force Canada into acting, at least tacitly, within NATO and possibly also in other international bodies as part of a North American bloc. There are certainly times when, because Canadian and American views and interests on an issue coincide, Canada wants to act together with the United States; but Canada has always been free to choose. A more consistent pattern of agreement or collaboration could create expectations on the part of the Americans that would increase their tendency to regard any difference as disloyalty. It could also diminish Canada's hand in international diplomacy by identifying Canada as a 'satellite' – a reputation which it does not have in international and professional circles, despite Canadian criticism to this effect.

It is doubtful that there would be much Canadian tone in the 'North American' voice, although Canada would have some leverage in areas where it had economic or strategic clout. The arrangement would essentially be a bargain in which Canada could demand some American concessions. A considerable difficulty, however, would be the persistent problem of getting commitments from the United States administration that would be honoured by Congress. The prospect of such an arrangement is not attractive, but if the range of choices is further limited by economic and technological factors, it might seem the lesser of two evils as the only way to influence American policy at all. Canada could deliberately choose this course, or it could drift into it through timidity or docility, or through the 'North American' media's gradual extinction of Canadian points of view. On the other hand, Canada might very well find that it too cannot afford the United States.

Does Canada's influence in the Alliance depend on the strength of its military contribution? Could Canada have more influence if it put more troops and material into the field? Most of the allies have taken a dim view of Canadian defence expenditures over the past decade or more, but there is little assurance that Canada would get its own way more often if it doubled its defence budget. On the other hand, removal of Canadian forces from Germany, except in the context of some agreed new shift in Alliance strategy, would pretty well rule Canada out of consideration altogether. If one lived in a political vacuum, one might suggest that the best way for Canada to get its allies to take it seriously would be to go neutral. This would be an idle threat, and not only because of American pressure; for many reasons – geographical, historical, and cultural – Canadians do not think neutral, perverse as this fact may seem in the eyes of many peace-loving citizens. Still, if Canada confronted its single-minded allies with the prospect that the largest country in the Alliance, and one with a long frontier exposed to Soviet power, might disengage from defence co-operation (however passive that co-operation might seem to have been), the allies would almost certainly give a gratifying shudder and would turn their eyes to the northwest. Canadians would be vilified, of course, but they would be noticed and perhaps even heard – that is, if they had anything to say except that they had been aggrieved.

To what extent might the NATO experience be adaptable elsewhere? Should Canada consider the need to belong to a security system in the Pacific? Canada is a Pacific power, and it is in the Pacific area rather than in Europe that Soviet encroachment might be more threatening. Indeed, there are more difficult problems of security looming in Asia than there are in Europe, where a balance has been achieved. The West Coast of North America is in the NATO area; it is covered in the NORAD provisions; its defence is often discussed in the Canada–United States Permanent Joint Board on Defence (PJBD); Canadian and United States naval forces co-operate with each other; and there has been much exchange of views and information in the NATO Council on what is going on in the Pacific.

Is the time ripe for some sort of Pacific security community? It need not be like NATO; it could be something that fitted the very different configuration of powers in the Pacific rim. There are good reasons for Canada to become active in this direction since, with the coalescing of Europe, Canada could be left out in the cold. Moreover, it would be good for Canada to create institutions and linkages covering its varied interests with countries from Japan to New Zealand.

Looking at the question of Canada having specific security commitments across the Pacific casts some light on the broader question of the role of the smaller members of NATO outside the designated area. Canada might well consider that security in the Persian Gulf or the Indian Ocean is as important to Canadians as to Americans or Britons, though it has always been hard to figure out what Canada could do about it. While major powers could send their fleets or could provide non–United Nations peacekeeping forces, Canada could only send forces that would have to be incorporated into those of the larger powers, and it would have only nominal control over their use and might not be in total agreement with the foreign policies that its forces were implementing. For a lesser power, the advantage of a body like NATO is that it provides a framework into which a country can fit its forces in accordance with agreed rules of command and with provision for some voice in determining a common policy. While there is no ideal formula for an alliance, this has seemed the best available solution. However, it has been applicable only where the circumstances were right. It is hard to visualize any such alliance for collective defence among countries as disparate as Australia, China, and the Philippines. Certainly, it is easy to agree in general terms that Canada has both an interest in and a responsibility for security in the regions beyond its western coastline. But exactly what kind of military contribution could Canada make?

Should Canada's linkages in the Pacific and in Asia be framed in security institutions or in economic institutions? What could Canada contribute militarily? Its armed forces are already overstretched, and they are not likely to be expanded. Canada has very few ships and all of them have to be in the Atlantic under current commitments. Could Canada have any force in the Pacific without reducing its Atlantic commitment? In 1968, when the government sought to downplay its role in Europe and turn eastward, this was in order to seek a greater role in the Third World, but not a military role. One should also bear in mind that the strong cultural and historical ties with Europe would have their effect on priorities. (Canada, it might be noted, has in the past played its own kind of 'security' role in Asia by its heavy contribution to peacekeeping operations. Since Canada has no formal alignment in Asia, this might still be possible, but the long and frustrating experience of peacekeeping in Indochina has strengthened Canadian resistance to such roles when they are not under United Nations authority.)

The instinctive Canadian alignment with Western Europe, notable in 1914, 1939, and at the birth of NATO in 1948-49, is well illustrated in the Canadian role in the Conference on Security and Cooperation in Europe (CSCE).[6] When in June 1973 the government agreed to go to Helsinki, Canadians were not asked squarely whether they wanted a permanent commitment to maintain the security of a continent that was not their own. Perhaps it was taken for granted that this decision had been made in 1949, but that was an 'Atlantic' association, not a 'European' one. In a sense, Canada marched into the CSCE for a peripheral reason. The Russians were trying to set up a purely European security body, detached from the United States. In the face of this challenge, it seemed necessary for the North American members of NATO to go to Helsinki to prove that the United States could not be excluded. When Canada made the NATO commitment in 1949, it was hoped that this was a temporary necessity, but by the time the CSCE came around it seemed to have been decided that Canadians were Europeans for ever. Canada took the conference very seriously and has continued to do so. The active Canadian role in the planning conference provides evidence of a constructive role which, ironically, was to some extent attributable to Canada's odd-man-out position vis-à-vis the other groupings. The possibilities of the CSCE in the field of human rights, and its role in trying to bridge the social and cultural gaps between Eastern and Western Europe, have appeared more important to Canada than any military implications. The security role of the CSCE, however, is not so much in any specific military provisions as in its function of institutionalizing détente.

As explained by Louis Rogers, who led the Canadian delegation to the lengthy second review meeting in Madrid in 1980-83, the CSCE works on an incremental basis, establishing agreements by starting from modest beginnings and then building on them in successive steps. While the 1975 Final Act of Helsinki was a far from perfect document, it did establish an outline to which all thirty-five participating states could subscribe. It was further extended in Madrid, where the negotiations took longer than those which had led to the Final Act itself. The reason for this was the worsening of East-West relations and also the heightened ideological tension that was consciously brought to the meeting. Nevertheless, the Madrid negotiations were an undoubted success (within the limits of the CSCE process which, on the basis of the pattern set in the Final Act itself, means that implementation is good when East-West relations are good and that they are poor when East-West relations are poor), but the success was obscured by the Korean Air Lines incident, which occurred a week before the meeting wound up.

The concluding document of Madrid contained provision for tackling one of the two bases on which there was a possibility of nuclear war: a miscalculation starting in the conventional field (the other basis being a misunderstanding in the nuclear field). This might come about either from one side misunderstanding what the other side was doing or from a mistaken belief that there was an opportunity for gain by conventional means. In such circumstances, if the attacker seemed to be facing failure or if the defender could not cope, the side which stood at risk of losing would probably resort to the use of nuclear weapons. The Madrid session sought to make it difficult for either side to resort to surprise attack; it required the reporting of military activities in such a way that explanation could be demanded about any deviation from what could be regarded as 'normal activity.' Refusal to explain would, of course, warn the intended victim. The same set of measures would make the misinterpretation of ordinary activity unlikely.

If such 'confidence-building' measures could be agreed upon, large military forces – conventional or nuclear – would lose much of their attraction, and this should make actual measures of the reduction of forces more desirable. In short, over time there might be a real inducement to governments to reduce those forces that were not serving a political purpose. This might sound somewhat idealistic, but tackling the problem the other way round has not succeeded so far.

Much of this, maybe all of it, would depend on an improved international climate. Each side must feel that its security interests are being given equal consideration and are being taken properly into account. In other words, neither party should be made to feel that it, or its right to survive according to its own ideological system, is under threat. Challenges to the theoretical legitimacy of the Soviet system have been shown to induce heightened nervousness in the ruling class and to make the Soviets dig in their heels and refuse compliance, thus frustrating the search for a *modus vivendi* – or, as the East would say, peaceful coexistence.

To what extent is the CSCE really serving any useful purpose? Breaking up the institution at this time would be dangerously destabilizing. But might there come a point when one should resort to ridicule and break off the process? In Mr Rogers's view, the Europeans would not permit this. The process itself is of great importance to them, and they would probably refuse to end it even if there were no agreement at all. As long as the Soviet Union is willing to continue the process, it should go on.

The experience of the review meetings in both Belgrade and Madrid has suggested that the West may have to make a choice. On the one hand, it can lower the level of criticism and seek to gain the maximum performance possible under the 1975 agreements and seek to expand that area of agreement in accordance with the practice of gradual, incremental improvements. Alternatively, the West can have the undoubted pleasure of criticism up to whatever level of severity it pleases, but in the certain knowledge that little will be achieved in the way of practical results. There is no way in which a power like the USSR can be forced to do what it does not want to do. It is perhaps noteworthy that substantial emigration from the USSR was permitted when détente was apparently in good repair; but in the course of three years of pounding, the Russians evolved a philosophical justification of their behaviour which satisfied them, even if it did not convince others. Meanwhile, the West made its own job harder by encouraging the adoption of such philosophical defences.

In the international institutions through which the West seeks security, the CSCE has taken its place among the older United Nations and NATO, whose security role was discussed earlier. The balance of this chapter returns to these more traditional institutions and to their interrelationship.[7]

Major changes have taken place in the security system that was evolved after World War II. As Peter Dobell pointed out, initially the United Nations and NATO 'covered the world.' In Korea, for example, the United Nations provided an institutional cover for a major American-led military operation outside Europe. Not until Vietnam did the limits on the postwar system for control of international affairs become evident. These included, first of all, the extension of Soviet military power round the world. This was not entirely new; as early as 1956, the Czechs had provided weapons to Egypt. But the contemporary use of surrogates, such as Cuba which is by no means a major power, has been staggering. Secondly, there has been the independence of the Third World and the competitive arms trade. Local conflicts used to be snuffed out when the participants ran out of munitions, but this is no longer the case, as is apparent from the Iran-Iraq war. In 1982 Argentina, with French weapons, could put Great Britain at considerable risk. A 'power' can no longer look after the world.

The old technique, leaving it in practice for one member of NATO to act, as in the case of France in Chad, has become increasingly difficult. The United States action in Grenada may have made it easier, from the American perspective, to settle differences in Central America. No doubt, if Washington had consulted NATO, it would not have got agreement on the action to be taken and the process would have taken too long. Yet should not NATO be the instrument for co-ordinating Western actions round the world? In Lebanon, the ill-fated interventions of the United States, France, Italy, and Britain were not co-ordinated. Action was ad hoc and there was no unified command. To some extent, the Economic Summit of the seven filled a void in handling matters outside the NATO area. It had the advantage that it included Japan and also that it involved top political leaders in its decisions and recommendations. Its disadvantage was that there was no institutional follow-up.

Looking at the scene from a Washington perspective, William Maynes has argued that United States support for either the United Nations or NATO will never return to its former levels. The United States will no longer act as a surrogate for a United Nations which itself cannot reach sufficient agreement to act without the United States. The result is a system with no one in charge. In the United States there is a problem of perception. Americans know that their country's capacity to do things is now limited, but they have not adjusted to the shattering of the three key postwar pillars of United States power: strategic superiority, control of the international monetary system, and dominance of the world's energy supplies. Forgotten also is the atmosphere of fear in which the North Atlantic Treaty was created after the Czech coup, a fear that was given substance by the Korean War. Because Soviet reality has changed from that of the 1950s, today's crisis is not like earlier crises. There is currently an increase in international lawlessness, and the cumulative impact has been damaging. There is no equilibrator. This role used to be played by the United States – but no longer. Instead, President Reagan has waged a great attack on international institutions and has scarred international principles, acting recklessly diplomatically, as in the pulling out of UNESCO and the Law of the Sea. The Alliance could tolerate one maverick, as it tolerated France under de Gaulle, but it cannot tolerate as mavericks either the United States or Germany.

What can be done in a situation in which the United States appears to be on a maverick course and yet needs allies to counter its persistent nightmare of another Pearl Harbor? What, in particular, can the West do about the United Nations and NATO? Maynes argued that since the United Nations is a liberal institution, one can often find common denominators among its members if one tries hard enough. On the other hand, if the United Nations is allowed to become a Third World organization, it is doomed. No one would want to pay for an organization that is perceived as belonging to someone else. There has to be a better balance between the voting strength and the financial strength. To save the United Nations, the West will have to get tough, but it needs a positive agenda for change, not a destructive one like Reagan's. Reform should be demanded, with the threat of financial withdrawal if there is no reasonable response to this demand. The allies of the United States should be pressing the Reagan administration harder, and they should also be letting the United States stand alone when it is being stubborn.

As for NATO, more European autonomy is required and better relations between the United States and the Soviet Union. The United States is no longer strong enough to offer the Europeans absolute assurances, so the Europeans must set out to protect themselves or must try harder to get on with the USSR. Finally, there will be no fundamental change in American foreign policy towards the Soviet Union until there is progress on the Middle East issue. It is poisoning relations with the USSR as well as with others, and is making foreign policy stagnant.

Given the widespread criticism of United States policies vis-à-vis international institutions and the recognition that its unilateralism is a danger sign, how can Western countries apply pressure? Maynes believes that there is a case for more co-ordinated action. While it was agreed in 1982 that UNESCO was in a scandalous state, there was no consensus for common action. In such institutions, action should not be left only to the United States because of its greater degree of financial control. Other countries could take the lead diplomatically from time to time. When the United States takes the action, the issue too often becomes polarized so that it is transformed into a Cold War issue on which the Eastern bloc automatically opposes and the non-aligned abstain. Such action also enhances the false notion that good causes are an American property. When the Americans let Moslem and other Third World states take the lead in the Assembly debate on Afghanistan, the result was a thumping defeat of the Russians. Might it not have been wiser to let the Koreans or the Japanese take the lead over the KAL disaster?

It is usually taken for granted that Canada's influence in international security institutions has declined considerably since the postwar years. Yet Canada has recently been reclassified as a 'foremost power' or as a 'principal power.'[8] In assessing the significance of these terms, Harald von Riekhoff has argued that Canada has made three major contributions to these institutions: it played a major part in the creation of the United Nations and in bringing NATO to life; secondly, Lester Pearson pursued a significant initiative in changing the Security Council's role from enforcement to peacekeeping; and, finally, Pierre Trudeau launched a so-called peace initiative. The last was somewhat more ephemeral than the other two. In the first two cases Canada worked with partners in a collective action, but Mr Trudeau acted on his own. He had a weaker starting point and was preaching to the superpowers, and there was less likelihood of any institutional consequence of his actions. What he undertook was to remind world leaders of the importance of détente, and in this sense it was a retrospective proposal rather than an initiative in the strict sense.

Professor von Riekhoff shares the general view that it is through the United Nations and NATO that Canada can most effectively participate, though he feels that there are some possible alternatives. One might be an expansion of the agenda of the Economic Summit of the seven, of which Canada is a member. He does not feel that a Pacific security institution, as discussed earlier, looks very promising.[9] As for the United Nations, it is an axiom that if there is to be effective action the superpowers must abstain, which is unlikely, or they must co-operate, which is improbable, though there have been exceptions such as the setting up of the United Nations Force in Cyprus. Canadian participation in peacekeeping in the future may be less likely, because of declining public support and the lack of adequate military resources. Enforcement action by the United Nations is extremely unlikely, but not impossible (if, for instance, there was a hostage-taking crisis with a strong humanitarian urge to do something).

Looking at the controversial question of Canada's influence, Dobell has argued that international influence is a matter of the total resources that are put into it. It is not strictly a matter of the quality of Canadian representation. Nor is it ideas that are needed, as Mr Trudeau implied. This is not the root of Canada's problem. Rather, it is a lack of standing. When Canada brings little to the table, it cannot expect to be listened to. The way Canada is perceived is important. Even if Canada were to be perceived as simply trying to do its best, this could give it greater credibility. Canada could modestly increase its military capability and could offer advice in areas where it has some special qualification. For instance, in the Middle East, Canada has had a long experience in various kinds of peacekeeping as well as in United Nations diplomacy, and there it should try to be helpful. In making these suggestions, Dobell was aware that he was not offering a popular prescription. It was too much like advocating what has been scorned as 'quiet diplomacy.' As for the 'danger' of Europe coalescing and making Canada the odd man out, there could be advantages in this if the Europeans would look after themselves somewhat more effectivly, allowing Canada to play a larger role elsewhere.

NOTES

1 I am indebted to John G. H. Halstead for this formulation.
2 See above, Gerald Wright, 'Canada and the Reform of NATO,' p. 114 f.
3 Address to the joint session of the Irish Parliament, 4 June 1984; in United States *Department of State Bulletin* 84, no 2089 (August 1984), 17-18.
4 Communiqué issued following the ministerial meeting 9-10 December 1982 in *Texts of Communiqués and Declarations Issued after Meetings Held at Ministerial Level During 1982* (Brussels nd), 31.
5 I am indebted for this comment to Ian Smart, who was recently asked to contribute to a book being prepared in Europe, entitled *Can We Afford the United States?*
6 See Robert Spencer, ed., *Canada and the Conference on Security and Cooperation in Europe* (Toronto 1984).
7 The following pages draw heavily on the views expressed by three distinguished observers of the international scene, of very different backgrounds. Peter Dobell, director of the Ottawa-based Parliamentary Centre for Foreign Policy and Foreign Trade, formerly served with the Department of External Affairs; Professor Harald von Riekhoff is chairman of the Department of Political Science at Carleton University; and William Maynes, currently editor of the Washington quarterly *Foreign Policy*, was formerly with the United States State Department.
8 John Kirton and David Dewitt, *Canada: A Principal Power* (Toronto 1983).
9 See above, John W. Holmes, 'Canada, NATO, and Western Security,' pp. 130-32.

JOHN W. HOLMES

6 Conclusion: Security and Survival

What conclusions can be drawn about a global security system, and in particular about how Canada should fit into it? It is notable that in the foregoing discussion of international security institutions there are almost no proposals for new institutions or for the drastic recasting of those that exist. This can hardly be called complacency, for the discussion reflects an uneasiness about the state of existing structures. It may also suggest a determination to avoid glib solutions. However, there is little doubt of the need for institutions, and this means the comprehensive United Nations system, NATO, and the CSCE. It also means the Warsaw Treaty Organization (WTO), the Organization of American States (OAS), the Organization for African Unity (OAU), and the non-aligned movement, for there are areas in which security would be better maintained, where possible, by non-Western bodies. This prescription should, on the whole, be evolutionary rather than revolutionary – eclectic in the search for varying ways and means rather than for global 'solutions.' Nevertheless, the global balance has to be borne in mind constantly by all the powers. The fear of a drift into anarchy, with the erosion of hard won international principles,

is basic. Threats come, no doubt, from the various international man-
ifestations of communism, from the threatened and by no means
unjustified revolt of the Third World masses, and from the increasing
resort to terrorism as a weapon of change. There is also the threat to
internationalism of revolutionary nationalism, the virulent kind as
seen in western Asia and also the nostalgic kind as seen among the
great powers, with the resurgence of protectionism and a mood of
defiance towards international régimes. Closer to home there is worry
about a petulant nationalism or continentalism and the fading of a
truly international perspective on Canada's real interests in peace and
security.

But Canadians have to examine their own assumptions. Have
they cultivated a blind faith in international institutions? Have they
been so bemused by this conviction, to which they were converted
by World War II, that multilateralism has become a substitute for
policy? Gerald Wright[1] has provocatively raised the question, pointing
out that Canada's history within the Commonwealth, and later in its
relationship with a great power neighbour, has led Canadians to faith
in the formula of independence secured within multilateral associations. It is a good question. It was in the interest of Canadian nationalism that Canadians needed internationalism. For a century or
so they have been absorbed by the search for ways of expressing their
own opinions and exerting influence on world events that touch them.
Has the formula become the message? One might recall the faith in
the resonance of the slogan 'collective security' as a guarantee of peace
that prevented Canadians from a realistic defence policy, with arms
for collective security, until aggression had actually occurred in Korea
in 1950.

Since then, of course, Canadians have learned that international
institutions are not mechanisms on which countries can cast their
burdens and that each member has to work hard to gain its ends and
to keep the body propelling instead of stagnating. As a result of the
experience, Canadians moved away from the illusion of world government towards something like collective management. Even this
concept, which propelled Canada to crusading zeal in the United
Nations Conference on the Law of the Sea, has been seriously eroded
by the rejection of a minimal seabed authority by major Western

powers and the Soviet Union. The Canadian reach for joint management, on a bilateral basis, of the East Coast fisheries was spurned by the United States Congress. A sympathetic American scholar, Charles Doran, has commented that 'the East Coast Fisheries Treaty, its ambitious proposals for joint management and the very conception of reciprocal access itself were all perhaps residuals of an earlier, less sovereignty conscious era.'[2] In the evolving structure of NORAD, it might be noted, Canada and the United States have moved towards defining separate jurisdictions. Faith in co-operation, belief in the essentiality of international law and regulation remain, but the noble idea of international management has certainly declined since Canada seriously thought in the late 1940s that there could be United Nations 'management' of atomic energy. Have Canadians grown wiser and more discriminating or more cynical? If they are to confront the hard-nosed cynics, they will have to be pretty hard-nosed about the international institutions they sponsor.

What seems lacking in international institutions of whatever kind is the sense of coherence, the leadership which was found in the exhilarating period when the new world order was being fashioned, however ingenuously. Nostalgia, however, serves no purpose because the world has changed – or at least our comprehension of its nature has been greatly sensitized and complicated. The kind of uneasy equilibrium we have maintained for forty years is in danger. Things could go downhill rapidly if we lose our way. It is futile, for example, just to go on saying that a system of deterrence has kept the peace for forty years and ought not to be disturbed. This is at best a partial truth because deterrence is itself inconstant. The challenge is to adjust to the shifting redistribution of power in the world, to control it rather than arrest it. Power, furthermore, has to be estimated functionally, not just as the gross possession of either economic or military resources, but as the capacity, unilaterally or multilaterally, to apply it effectively. We need to reconsider the very concept of leadership.

With an eye on the balance, the changing role of the United States is always a focus of concern, particularly if its capacity and its will for global management is declining. Deploring the attitude of the Reagan administration comes easily, but Reagan-bashing is not enough.

United States leadership has always been resented; but from a Canadian point of view, at least, it was better than no leadership at all, and it has come to be expected. Collective leadership seems essential in the new situation, but it is a good deal harder to achieve in all the institutions under consideration. The Reaganites, with their unilateral attitude on collective action or decision, do not make the transition easy, but the rest of us have to understand that it is not only United States power but also United States responsibility that has to be shared. How to do that on strategic arms limitation, for example, or on conflict prevention outside the NATO area, is more than a simple moral issue.

We in the West have taken for granted for some time that United States power in the world is declining, not absolutely but relatively, and that we must adjust to this historical fact. It is a view constantly stressed by Americans themselves and ought not to be regarded as anti-American, for they do not necessarily deplore the phenomenon. However, the Reagan administration does not appear to share this view, except as a simple expectation of more loyal support from allies for strategic decisions taken in Washington. Perhaps the assumption does require re-examination. If those in charge in Washington think that they have retained undisputed world leadership, then this is by no means a negligible element in the equation. That the assumption may be built on quicksand is, however, another calculation we must make. Militarily, the United States and the Soviet Union are still in a class by themselves and are drawing farther away from the rest of us all the time. A question of the institutional relationship, as noted in this book, is whether the rest of us can afford to keep military company with them. Another question is whether their power is too ungainly to be used with the precision required for the great power management of international security that was envisaged in the United Nations Charter.

Economic statistics certainly indicate declining power, relatively, of the superpowers, but what is to be made of the unexpected resurgence of the United States economy? What kind of factor is that strength in the international system now? In the past it was a firm basis for an expanding international economy and a world system. However, if current interest rates, congressional protectionism, and a sour view of economic institutions are an indication, will the United

States be a factor of a very different kind, a spoiler rather than a builder of international systems? There may be reason for optimism in the United States' need for allies and its inescapable dependence on, among other things, an orderly trading and financial system. Five years' exposure to the realities of international life have modified some of the reckless assumptions of a very provincial team. At the same time, unilateral actions in the Middle East and in Central America have been disconcertingly unsuccessful. Banking crises in Latin America and a critical imbalance in United States trade encouraged greater interest in the health of the International Monetary Fund (IMF) and the General Agreement on Tariffs and Trade (GATT). The importance of Alliance support in negotiating with the Russians became clear, along with the need to go to Geneva.

A disturbing fact, of which the rulers in Washington have been too little aware, is that although Americans may have been standing tall again in their own eyes, hostility to and fear of the United States have been more widespread than at any time since 1776. Good democrats abroad have been less inclined than in the past to look to the United States for inspiration, and Washington has become a bogey, its sins exaggerated by the lore of CIA omnipotence and Wall Street arrogance. Mindless anti-Americanism of the kind found in Iran or Libya and in much revolutionary rhetoric (as distinct from legitimate criticism of American policies) is a dangerous anarchical force loose in the world. It has done much to strangle rational debate in United Nations bodies, and unfortunately it has been encouraged of late by the behaviour of the United States. This is a cause of worry not only for Americans but for all who regard dedicated and constructive American participation as being essential to the equitable and effective operation of international institutions. As one of President Reagan's disillusioned representatives, at a late session of the Law of the Sea Conference, lamented: 'Once leadership is abdicated and the world finds that it can proceed without us, it will not be easy for the United States to reclaim its influence.'[3]

In these circumstances, Canadian delegations have been seeking to play a 'damage-limiting' role. It is wise not to call this a role of mediator, a term used too often in the past and implying too formal a vocation. The requirement for the friends and allies of the United

States is primarily diplomatic, using whatever advantages they may have in particular circumstances to avert confrontation, to grope towards agreement, to avoid action which would weaken the structures, and to shun stridency, while recognizing, of course, that in some things Alliance solidarity is essential. There is a public prejudice against 'quiet diplomacy,' but in practice there is very often 'no other way.' The United Nations and other institutions are not international governments; they are instruments for multilateral diplomacy, and they are best strengthened by improving the quality of the diplomacy.

Canadian avoidance of the denunciatory posture is partly a nice calculation of tactics, but when dealing with the United States it is also based on the confidence that in the end the more enlightened internationalists have usually triumphed in the great republic. If this were not so, Canada would not exist. There is real worry whether irreparable damage may be done, to the United Nations in particular, before United States attitudes have switched back from negative to constructive. To argue effectively, however, Canadians have to recognize the partial validity of American grievances. It is easier for Canadians to see the importance of international structures because, unlike the Americans, they cannot embrace the illusion of going it alone. The tempting delusion for some Canadians, however, is that North America might go it alone, and from this perspective they tend to identify themselves with the American sceptics. In the light of such prevalent scepticism, it is reassuring to learn from a Gallup poll of March 1985 that 83 per cent of Canadians think it is important to make the United Nations a success.

As might be expected of a group of Canadians in the mid-1980s, the approach to international structures reflected in this volume is more functionalist than utopian. The search has been for those ways and means which have worked and on which we might build. The concern over United States policy is less a resentment of its arrogance than worry over the lack of its ballast in institutions that have to be reshaped. At the same time, there is a recognition that American stubbornness over some of the obvious abuses of the system is not only justified – to some extent, at least – but could also serve a purpose in the restoration of a realistic equilibrium. There is an argument, therefore, for the pursuit of an improved international system by the

Western powers, not in unison but by variant tactics. Because Canada and the other smaller allies are less fearsome, they could help in the search for compromise between an aroused Third World and an aroused and rather angry United States, although it would be singularly unwise to proclaim any such intention.

While unachievable proposals for a new international economic order have to be resisted, the need for rapid change must be acknowledged. Despair of any improvement in developing countries might be the greatest threat to peace and security. It could, of course, unite the North, for the Soviet bloc, while exploiting the anti-Western bias of the South, has just as much reason as the West to fear anarchical violence. In 1984, Mr Chernenko suggested, in the context of the Ethiopian famine and the move to arms control negotiations, that East and West might better be combining their efforts to aid the Third World. This suggestion may only have been a propaganda ploy and too sensible to be taken seriously, but it is the type of opening that ought not to be ignored. Even if the chances of success are small, might one not hope that the increasing challenge of global hunger and deprivation would force international institutions into co-operative programs in which Eastern and Western countries learned to work together? (Indeed, this did happen in Ethiopia.) Then we might see the kind of international infrastructure which, even if it could not guarantee the outlawing of war, would at least be a powerful practical force in discouraging it. This is, in any case, a better working philosophy than despair.

This kind of functionalism is somewhat more sophisticated than the 'functionalism' advocated by David Mitrany and others before and during the last war, according to which the hope of peace was in the interdependence created by the interlocking of economic interests among nations.[4] It has become customary to discredit Mitrany by pointing out that increasing interdependence on a global scale and the existence of many functioning international economic institutions have not brought peace to the world. The verdict in the long run, however, remains to be heard. Ian Smart points out that the diminution of violence in relations among industrialized countries is attributable not only to the costs of war but also to the benefits that can be enjoyed by not engaging in war.[5] In any case, it can be argued that although increased interdependence is in itself no guarantee of peaceful coexistence, there can be no peace unless, alongside institutions to cope with military security, there are those which, however unsuccessfully, try to deal with the economic and social issues that threaten to overwhelm us. Security is now seen as a much wider problem for the members of the United Nations than just forestalling armed aggression or stopping fights. This two-pronged approach was in fact the kind of functionalism enshrined in the United Nations Charter and is its major advance over the League of Nations.

In 1945 there was hope that economic questions could be kept free of political considerations, but this is one of the many illusions we have worked through in the instructive experience over four decades of international institutionalization. Because national and international politics are to an increasing extent concerned with economic and social questions, and rightly so, the economic and social bodies have naturally been 'politicized.' It is not the fact but the nature of the politicization that is cause for concern. The global dimensions of security in this multifarious sense are not easy to grasp and hold, but in any study of the institutions for peace and security – especially those institutions that deal in the more traditional sense with peacemaking and peacekeeping, and the control of deadly weapons – one must bear in mind the widening ramifications of 'security.'

In the early postwar years the traditional 'political and security' bodies were regarded as the primary *raison d'être* of the system. We tend now to take a more functional and less hierarchical view of priorities. Each has its value, and there is no need to rank them. Nevertheless, the public still judge the system, particularly the United Nations, by its capacity to keep the peace, without fully realizing that peace is a by-product. They tend to judge this capacity by what Ian Smart has called the wrong criterion; that is, success in producing an international society free of violence and conflict. By such a standard, our institutions have seemed to fail, and the lack of confidence in them has become part of the problem. Ernst Haas, who once described the search for world order as 'nothing but an attempt to conquer turbulence,' has concluded that the toleration of relatively low levels of conflict is a lesson that has been learned. No conflict that threatens the system of independent states has emerged since 1945, and even the Cold War has been managed, at least until now:

Governments in the 1970s have learned to tolerate a level of conflict that does not threaten the system as a whole, while the United Nations and regional organizations continue to be effective in abating many conflicts and settling a few. Regime decay is not incompatible with learning lessons at another level of consciousness. The toleration of conflict that remains diffused, confined to weak states and removed to the periphery of politics and geography, may be a second-best solution to the problem of war. But it is better than making every conflict a matter of principle.[6]

It may be recalled that one of the objections raised in Canada and some other countries to the principle of universal collective security, as espoused first in the League of Nations, was that in practice it would mean the escalation of conflict by making small wars universal. This seemed too much like what happened in 1914, when a petty assassination in the Balkans entrapped all the great powers. That is really why we have the veto in the Security Council of the United Nations. The veto, as Inis Claude describes it, is like the fuse in an electric circuit, designed to break the flow when continued operation would be dangerous. In his view, 'the veto is not so much a means by which a great power may protect its interests as a device for protecting the collective system.'[7]

If international institutions are to remain effective, should we not temper utopian expectations? Those who are not prepared to write off the human race are inclined, in the face of those who condemn our present institutions because they have not ended all violence, to defend somewhat indiscriminately the United Nations and other institutions and all their works. They ignore many of the gross realities of international politics by declaring them unacceptable and calling rather simply for conferring on institutions more and more authority to do things beyond any possible consensus. Many think that sin in the world can be shouted down and they regard the consideration of tactics to contain it as immoral. If our rudimentary world order is to survive and grow, examination of its institutions must begin with a ruthless facing of the facts of life on a refractory planet. But this means that we not only analyse the failures but also search for those things that have worked reasonably well, for methods that have promise.

The lapidary approach to the building of institutions is eternal. There is no 'solution' at the end, no framework that will guarantee perpetual peace. The experimentation must go on and on. Peace must be preserved from generation to generation in various mysterious ways, taking into consideration, among other things, changing technology, the rise and transformation of empires, shifts of economic strength, and the health of the planet. In this organic approach there is a danger of sounding Whiggish or Darwinian by describing change as progress. If we are to profit from experience, it is hard not to look at it this way, and it is possibly wise to do so as a working rule. Provided one does not rest in the illusion of a final solution, one can think of this process as a continuing adaptation to changing environments and circumstances, and not necessarily as 'progress.' Nevertheless, to stress the importance of precedent, of the need for growing respect for norms of international behaviour, one must sound something like a cautious Whig. The consideration given in detail to the problems of institutions for peace and security have certainly confirmed Ian Smart's introductory warning that 'a measure of order can only be preserved by constant and uncommonly skilful effort.' It has also confirmed his belief that although the strains within the international system have increased, 'there is encouragement to be drawn from the largely unheralded ways in which international behaviour has already been moderated, offsetting that disorderly trend.'[8] The principal reason for international institutions, as Leon Gordenker pointed out, is to institutionalize norms to limit certain aggressive actions. Although they have certainly not succeeded totally in that effort, it is encouraging to note the number of norms over the broad United Nations system, which have been accepted because member states recognize their own interests in such limitations.

The United Nations system may wither, but it is not likely to go quietly away. Even those who regret its birth might hesitate over the destabilizing effect of its demise. It has become embedded in the expectations of the peoples of the world. We use it astutely or fight a rearguard action against it. Above all, the United Nations should not be seen as sufficient unto itself, and it has in fact learned to accommodate itself to other bodies for peace and security more comfortably than the founders contemplated. The first major alteration in the security system, the creation of NATO in 1949, set the pattern by a deliberate decision to erect a supplementary system under Article 51 of the Charter, rather than an alternate system. Since then, the powers and practices of United Nations bodies have changed to such an extent that we have grown to think in terms of working with them, not in place of them. Still, the more one looks at the possibilities for regional or other special institutions, the more one recognizes the essentiality of an institution with aspirations to universality. It is the gathering threat to this assumption that leads to present bewilderment. How can we adjust the system to prevent powerful states from opting out?

Of course, it may happen that the problem of survival will loom more important than the preservation of peace and that the need for international discipline will be seen in a more powerful light. The functionalists could be proved right after all. In addition to military and economic security, we talk increasingly of 'environmental security.' Our hidden agenda is resource depletion, desertification, imminent shifts in climate, and pollution of the air and water on an epidemic scale. Although it attracted few headlines, there has been an international agreement straddling the porous Iron Curtain to counter the threat to the ozone layer. Canada and the Soviet Union have agreed to discuss their common problem of acid rain. So have the East and West Germans. It was the perception of a common threat which once brought the NATO nations into alliance and which, much later, brought the East and the West to Vienna and Geneva to negotiate arms control. The struggle for survival could require global regulation that is much tougher than that of our present institutions for peace and security – as ruthless, for example, as the Chinese attack on the birth rate. It took a couple of very bloody wars to produce the United Nations, and it may take some frightful disasters like the African famine to create what is required to deal with 'environmental security.' The Cold War would seem increasingly irrelevant if there were no more forests in Europe. On the other hand, one must warily realize that the threat from nature could stir passions which might soon lead us into black anarchy. Will order or chaos prevail? Opting for order is the obvious choice, but it is an exhausting project.

NOTES

1 Vice-president of the Donner Canadian Foundation and president of the Atlantic Council of Canada.

2 Charles Doran, *Forgotten Partnership* (Baltimore 1984), 203.
3 Leigh S. Ratiner, 'The Law of the Sea: A Crossroads for American Foreign Policy,' *Foreign Affairs* 60, no 5 (Summer 1982), 1021.
4 David Mitrany, *A Working Peace System* (New York 1946).
5 See above, Ian Smart, 'The International System: Will Chaos or Order Prevail?' pp. 15-16.
6 Ernst B. Haas, 'Regime Decay: Conflict Management and International Organizations, 1945-81,' *International Organization* 37, no 2 (Spring 1983), 235.
7 Inis Claude, *Swords into Ploughshares* (New York 1971), 156-57.
8 See above, Smart, 'The International System,' p. 33.

Select Bibliography

BERTRAM, CHRISTOPH. 'Europe and America in 1983,' *America and the World*, special issue of *Foreign Affairs* 62, no 2, 1984.

BOULDING, K.E. *The Image: Knowledge in Life and Society*. Ann Arbor: University of Michigan Press 1961.

BULL, HEDLEY. 'European Self-Reliance and the Reform of NATO,' *Foreign Affairs* 61, no 4 (Spring 1983), 874-92.

BYERS, R.B., et al. *Canada and Western Security: The Search for New Options*. Toronto: Atlantic Council of Canada 1982.

CANADA. DEPARTMENT OF EXTERNAL AFFAIRS. *Statement 86/30. Notes for a Speech by the Right Honourable Joe Clark, Secretary of State for External Affairs, at the Centre for International Studies, University of Toronto, 22 May 1986*.

CANADA. PARLIAMENT. *Interdependence and Internationalism: Report of a Special Joint Committee of the Senate and the House of Commons on Canada's International Relations*. Ottawa: Supply and Services Canada 1986.

CANADA. PARLIAMENT. HOUSE OF COMMONS. *Debates*. Ottawa: Supply and Services Canada 1984.

CARRINGTON, LORD. 'The Alastair Buchan Memorial Lecture,' *Survival* 25, no 4 (July/August 1983), 146-64.

CLAUDE, INIS. *Swords into Ploughshares*. 4th edn. New York: Random House 1971.

DANKERT, PIETER. 'Europe Together, America Apart,' *Foreign Policy* 53 (Winter 1983-84), 18-33.

DORAN, CHARLES. *Forgotten Partnership: U.S.-Canada Relations Today*. Baltimore: Johns Hopkins University Press 1984.

EBAN, ABBA. *The New Diplomacy: International Affairs in the Nuclear Age*. New York: Random House 1983.

HAAS, ERNST B. 'Regime Decay: Conflict Management and International Organizations, 1945-81,' *International Organization* 37, no 2 (Spring 1983), 189-256.

HOLMES, JOHN W. 'The Dumbbell Won't Do,' *Foreign Policy* 50 (Spring 1983), 3-22.

INTERNATIONAL INSTITUTE FOR STRATEGIC STUDIES. *Strategic Survey 1983-1984*. London: International Institute for Strategic Studies 1984.

JOFFE, JOSEF. 'Europe's American Pacifier,' *Foreign Policy* 54 (Spring 1984), 64-82.

KIRTON, JOHN AND DEWITT, DAVID. *Canada: A Principal Power. A Study in Foreign Policy and International Relations*. Toronto: John Wiley 1983.

KISSINGER, HENRY. 'A Plan to Reshape NATO,' *Time*, 5 March 1984, 26-30.

MITRANY, DAVID. *A Working Peace System*. New York: Oxford University Press 1946.

NATO FINAL COMMUNIQUÉS 1949-74; 1982, 1983, 1984. Issued by Ministerial Sessions of the North Atlantic Council, the Defence Planning Committee, and the Nuclear Planning Group. Brussels: NATO Information Service, nd.

PEARSON, LESTER. 'The Development of Canadian Foreign Policy,' *Foreign Affairs* 30, no 1 (October 1951), 26.

RATINER, LEIGH S. 'The Law of the Sea: A Crossroads for American Foreign Policy,' *Foreign Affairs* 60, no 5 (Summer 1982), 1006-1021.

SCHWARTZ, DAVID N. *NATO's Nuclear Dilemmas*. Washington: The Brookings Institution 1983.

SMART, IAN. 'The Adopted Image: Assumptions about International Relations,' *International Journal* xxxix, no 2 (Spring 1984), 251-66.

SOHN, LOUIS. 'The Security Council's Role in the Settlement of International Disputes,' *American Journal of International Law* 78 (April 1984), 402-404.

SPENCER, ROBERT, ed. *Canada and the Conference on Security and Co-operation in Europe*. Toronto: Centre for International Studies 1984.

UNITED NATIONS. *Official Records of the General Assembly, Thirty-Seventh Session*. Supplement no 1 (A/37/1) 1982.

UNITED NATIONS. *Official Records of the Security Council. Resolutions and Decisions*. 1967, 1979, 1982 and 1983.

UNITED STATES. *Department of State Bulletin* 84, no 2089 (August 1984) 17-18.

Index